STATISTICA™

QUICK REFERENCE

StatSoft™

D1384630

STATSOFT SINGLE USER LICENSE AGREEMENT

The following constitutes the terms of the License Agreement between a single user (User) of this software package, and the producer of the package, StatSoft, Inc. (called Statsoft hereafter). By opening the package, you (the User) are agreeing to become bound by the terms of this agreement. If you do not agree to the terms of this agreement do not open the package, and contact the StatSoft Customer Service Department (or an authorized StatSoft dealer) in order to obtain an authorization number for the return of the package. This License Agreement pertains also to all third party software included in or distributed with StatSoft products.

License

The enclosed software package is sold to be used on one computer system by one user at a time. This License Agreement explicitly excludes renting or loaning the package, the use of this package on multiuser systems, networks, or any time sharing systems. (Contact StatSoft concerning Multiuser License Programs.) The user is allowed to make a backup copy for archival purposes and/or to install the software package on a hard disk. However, the software will never be installed on more than one hard disk at a time. The documentation accompanying this software package (or any of its parts) shall not be copied or reproduced in any form.

Disclaimer of Warranty

Although producing error free software is obviously a goal of every software manufacturer, it can never be guaranteed that a software program is actually free of errors. Business and scientific application software is inherently complex (and it can be used with virtually unlimited numbers of data and command settings, producing idiosyncratic operational environments for the software); therefore, the User is cautioned to verify the results of his or her work. This software package is provided "as is" without warranty of any kind. StatSoft and distributors of StatSoft software products make no representation or warranties with respect to the contents of this software package and specifically disclaim any implied warranties or merchantability or fitness for any particular purpose. In no event shall StatSoft be liable for any damages whatsoever arising out of the use of, inability to use, or malfunctioning of this software package. StatSoft does not warrant that this software package will meet the User's requirements or that the operation of the software package will be uninterrupted or error free.

Limited Warranty

If within 30 days from the date when the software package was purchased (i.e., invoice date), the program disks are found to be defective (i.e., they are found to be unreadable by the properly aligned disk drive of the computer system on which the package is intended to run), StatSoft will replace the disks free of charge. After 30 days, the User will be charged for the replacement a nominal disk replacement fee. If within 90 days from the date when the software package was purchased (i.e., invoice date), the software package was found by the User not capable of performing any of its main (i.e., basic) functions described explicitly in promotional materials published by StatSoft, StatSoft will provide the User with replacement disks free of defects, or if the replacement cannot be provided within 90 days from the date when StatSoft was notified by the User about the defect, the User will receive a refund of the purchasing price of the software package.

Updates, Corrections, Improvements

The User has a right to purchase all subsequent updates, new releases, new versions, and modifications of the software package introduced by StatSoft for an update fee or for a reduced price (depending on the scope of the modification). StatSoft is not obligated to inform the User about new updates, improvements, modifications, and/or corrections of errors introduced to its software packages. In no event shall StatSoft be liable for any damages whatsoever arising out of the failure to notify the User about a known defect of the software package.

QUICK REFERENCE

Detailed
Table of Contents

StatSoft™

StatSoft™

StatSoft™

StatSoft™

StatSoft™

StatSoft™

STATISTICA DATA FILES

Cases and variables. STATISTICA data are organized into cases and variables. If you are unfamiliar with this notation you can think of cases as the equivalent of records in a data base management program (or rows of a spreadsheet), and variables as the equivalent of fields (columns of a spreadsheet). Each case consists of a set of values of variables. For example, suppose 4 persons (cases) completed 3 tests; there may be a total of 5 variables in the data file: *Gender* (*Male*=male subject, *Female*=female subject), *Educat* (*C*=college, *H*=high-school), and 3 test scores (*Test1* through *Test3*). Shown below is a listing of such a file.

		1	2	3	4	5
Case		GENDER	EDUCAT	TEST1	TEST2	TEST3
J. Baker		MALE	C	12	345	12.30
A. Smith		MALE	H	13	454	13.60
M. Brown		FEMALE	H	13	433	13.70
C. Mayer		MALE	C	12	387	12.80

Data: TESTS.STA 5v * 4c — Data from three tests.

Case names. The first column in the file may contain names of cases (optional).

Text values. The two variables *Gender* and *Educat* contain text values. Internally, STATISTICA will reference text values in "double notation," that is, STATISTICA will assign numeric equivalents to those values; therefore, where applicable, you can perform all statistical analyses on those variables, as if they were numeric values. For example, suppose the program (or you) made the following assignments:

1 = *Male*, 2 = *Female* (for *Gender*); and

1 = *C*, 2 = *H* (for *Educat*).

You can switch between the two views of data (numeric or text) in the spreadsheet by pressing the *Text Values* (*ABC*) button on the spreadsheet toolbar.

After switching to numeric representation of text values, the file will look as follows:

		1	2	3	4	5
Case		GENDER	EDUCAT	TEST1	TEST2	TEST3
J. Baker		1	1	12	345	12.30
A. Smith		1	2	13	454	13.60
M. Brown		2	2	13	433	13.70
C. Mayer		1	1	12	387	12.80

Data: TESTS.STA 5v * 4c — Data from three tests.

"Double notation" of values (summary). As shown in the example (above), in STATISTICA, each value may have two identities: numeric (e.g., *1*) and text (e.g., *Male*). This double notation simplifies the use of text values.

For example, when entering data, you could enter the values *1* and *2* in variable *Gender* to refer to males and females, respectively. Later, you can type *Male* into any cell containing a *1*, and at the point when you complete this entry, all *1*'s in this column will automatically change to *Male*. In other words, because *1* did not have a text equivalent, the program will understand that you intended to assign the text value *Male* to *1* in this variable. You can repeat the same for *2* and *Female*.

This feature simplifies entering text values; at the same time you do not lose any advantages of using numeric data (they can still be used in subsequent numeric analyses). For more information, see *How to enter/edit the assignments between numeric and text values*, in the *Reference* section (page 89).

Other information about variables stored in STATISTICA data files. In addition to the raw data, STATISTICA system data files can also store other (optional) information related to individual variables, such as:

- display formats (e.g., the number of decimals or date-value formats),

- specific values which you intend to ignore in calculations (i.e., *Missing Data* codes),

- long variable names and comments,

StatSoft™

- long labels and comments attached to individual values,

- formulas which can be used to define, recode or transform each variable,

- dynamically-updated links between the data file and other Windows-compatible data files, that is, Windows *Dynamic Data Exchange* (DDE) links.

All those specifications of a variable can be accessed by double-clicking on the variable's name in the data spreadsheet.

Headers, comments. Each STATISTICA data file may also contain the following text identification:

- a one-line header information (displayed in the title area of the spreadsheet) which can be used to label reports, and

- multi-line comments or notes about the file (in the form of a paragraph of text).

Both types of information are accessible by double-clicking on the title area of the spreadsheet (or by selecting the *Header...* option in the pull-down menu *Edit*).

Colors, fonts, sizes. Also, all customizations of the appearance of the data file (such as column width and height, colors, or font) are stored along with the data and can be used, for example, to facilitate identifying specific files or data sets from specific projects.

StatSoft™

INTRODUCTORY EXAMPLE (AND OVERVIEW)

Installation

If you have not yet installed STATISTICA, please follow the instructions outlined below:

To install STATISTICA/w while running Windows, insert Disk 1 in drive A: and from the *File* menu select *Run*. Now type *A:SETUP* (you may use *B:SETUP* if appropriate for your system) and follow the instructions of the installation program. STATISTICA/w includes a complete on-line *electronic manual* (press *F1* at any point to access context-sensitive documentation).

Overview

Start the program by clicking on the STATISTICA *Basic Statistics and Tables* icon. The program will open (full-screen) and the last-used data file and the *Basic Statistics* startup panel will appear.

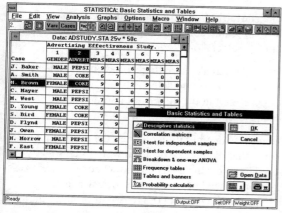

Customization of STATISTICA. Note that practically all aspects of the "behavior" and appearance of the program (even many elementary features illustrated in this example), can be permanently customized to match your preferences.

For example, even the first step (opening of the program) can be customized; you can change the default full-screen opening mode, the appearance of the startup panel, the appearance of the data spreadsheet, toolbars, etc.

Selecting a data file. STATISTICA automatically opens the last used file (*adstudy.sta* if you use the program for the first time) and you will see it in the data spreadsheet. If this example file is not found, you can open it using the pull-down menu *File* (or one of the *Open Data* buttons).

Data spreadsheet. The current data file is always displayed in the spreadsheet. Also, most output produced by STATISTICA is displayed in dynamic, spreadsheet-like tables called Scrollsheets (described below). However, the data spreadsheet is somewhat different from all output Scrollsheets in that it offers specific data management facilities.

For example, its toolbar contains the *Vars* (i.e., Variables) and *Cases* buttons which bring up options to restructure the data file (e.g., *Add, Move, Shift* variables).

Vars button menu: *Cases* button menu:

All those options are described in the section on the *Data Spreadsheet Toolbar* starting on page 33.

Variable specifications. The column names in the spreadsheet contain variable names. When you double-click on a column name, a *Variable Specifications* window will appear.

In this window, you can change the variable format, name, enter a formula to recalculate the values of the variable, link it to other files (via the Windows DDE conventions), etc. Specifications of all variables can also be reviewed and edited together in a "combined" variable specification window, accessible by pressing the All Specs button in this dialog or by pressing a toolbar button (see the second toolbar button from the left).

"Flying menus" in the spreadsheet. "Flying menus" are dynamic menus which are brought up by clicking with the right-mouse-button on an object (e.g., a cell in the spreadsheet).

A distinctive feature of the data spreadsheet (as compared to all output Scrollsheets, see below) is the options available from its flying menus.

When you click (using the right-mouse-button) on any cell of the spreadsheet, the menu which will pop up will include a selection of specific data base

management operations and other options related to the current variable (i.e., column) and/or case (i.e., row).

Calculating a correlation matrix. Now, compute a correlation matrix for the variables in the data file. If you have tried any of the spreadsheet options mentioned in the previous paragraphs or clicked on any other part of the screen, STATISTICA minimizes the startup panel, that is, it is reduced into a "floating" *Continue* button (see the bottom of the screen). To bring back the panel, simply double-click on the floating *Continue* button or press *Ctrl+S* (*S* for startup).

Once you have closed that panel using the *Cancel* button on the panel, you can re-open it by pressing *Ctrl+S* (*S* for startup) or by selecting the *Startup Panel* option from the pull-down menu *Analysis*.

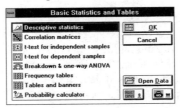

In the startup panel (or in the pull-down menu *Analysis*, which contains a copy of all the panel options), select *Correlation matrices*.

At this point, make sure that a block is not selected in the spreadsheet (to de-select a block, double-click on the "case" cell in the upper-left corner of the spreadsheet).

If there was one highlighted, then the program would assume that the block-variables were intentionally pre-selected for the analysis and when you later press *OK*, then instead of asking you for variables, as illustrated below, STATISTICA will produce the correlations for the block variables.

The *Pearson Product-Moment Correlation* dialog will appear.

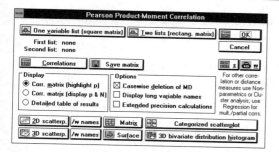

The _Variables_ button. This is a typical analysis definition dialog which contains options to specify the variables to be analyzed; this dialog also offers various output options. Every analysis definition dialog in STATISTICA contains at least one _Variables_ button which allows you to specify variables to be analyzed. You can click on it (or press _V_).

The "self-prompting" nature of all dialogs. All dialogs in STATISTICA also follow the "self-prompting" dialog convention, which means that whenever you are not sure what to select next, simply click _OK_ (or press _Alt+O_) and the program will proceed to the next logical step, asking you for the specific input if one is still missing (e.g., variables to analyzed).

The _Variable Selection_ window. When you click the _Variables_ button (or _OK_), a variable selection window will appear.

(Note that if you have "played" with the data spreadsheet before and selected a block, the variables highlighted in the block will automatically be selected, and when you press _OK_, the default

correlation matrix for the variables selected in the block will be produced.)

The _Variable Selection_ window supports various ways of selecting variables and it offers various shortcuts and options to review the contents of the data file. For example, you can _Spread_ the variable list to review their long labels, formulas or links; or you can _Zoom_ in on a variable (by pressing the _Zoom_ button) to review a sorted list of all its values and descriptive statistics for the variable.

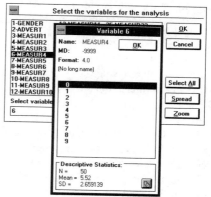

For this example, press the _Select All_ button, and then press _OK_ (twice) to generate a default correlation matrix for the selected variables. Note that instead of pressing the second _OK_, you could select a non-default output (e.g., some specialized graph or a custom format for the correlation matrix).

BASIC STATS	\multicolumn{8}{c}{Correlations [adstudy.sta]}
\multicolumn{8}{l}{Marked correlations are significant at p < .05000}								
\multicolumn{8}{l}{N=50 (Casewise deletion of missing data)}								
Variable	GENDER	ADVERT	MEASUR 1	MEASUR 2	MEASUR 3	MEASUR 4	MEASUR 5	MEASUR 6
GENDER	1.00	-.17	-.19	-.04	-.08	.02	.26	.05
ADVERT	-.17	1.00	-.03	.13	-.03	.11	-.28	-.15
MEASUR1	-.19	-.03	1.00	.01	-.11	.19	.04	-.01
MEASUR2	-.04	.13	.01	1.00	-.06	.01	.08	.15
MEASUR3	-.08	-.03	-.11	-.06	1.00	-.09	-.21	.14
MEASUR4	.02	.11	.19	.01	-.09	1.00	.10	-.16
MEASUR5	.26	-.28	.04	.08	-.21	.10	1.00	.23
MEASUR6	.05	-.15	-.01	.15	.14	-.16	.23	1.00
MEASUR7	-.37	.05	-.12	.05	.04	.01	-.05	.12
MEASUR8	-.04	-.02	-.02	-.08	-.19	.01	-.19	-.33
MEASUR9	-.15	.38	-.12	-.21	.21	.10	-.47	-.27
MEASUR10	.04	.03	-.15	.05	-.09	-.24	-.07	.13

Scrollsheets (dynamic output tables). The spreadsheet-like window in which the correlation

matrix is displayed (see above) is called a Scrollsheet (note that significant correlations are highlighted with a different color). Scrollsheets are used in STATISTICA to display most of the numeric output. They can hold anywhere from a short line to megabytes of output, and they offer a variety of options to facilitate reviewing the results and visualizing them in predefined and custom-defined graphs (see below).

Most of the Scrollsheet-control facilities are accessible via buttons on its toolbar (see page 44) and the "flying menus" (these menus can be brought up from every cell by pressing the right-mouse-button).

You can try these options to see how they work or review their descriptions by pressing the help key (*F1*) or double-clicking on the status bar (on the bottom of the STATISTICA window). For example, you can change all aspects of the display formats for each column, edit the output, append blank rows and columns to make room for notes or output pasted from other sources. Scrollsheets can be printed in a variety of ways (by default, in presentation-quality tables with high-resolution grid lines).

Scrollsheets can also be saved as:

- Scrollsheet documents (file name extension *.scr*) which can be opened later for reference or further analysis,

- standard STATISTICA input data files (file name extension *.sta*), so that output from one analysis can be used as input for another, or as

- text files.

Copy vs. Copy Raw.
Contents of Scrollsheets can be copied into the Clipboard via either *Copy Raw* (only the contents of the selected block) or the default *Copy* (the block along with its respective row and case names, by pressing *Ctrl+C*). If pasted into a word processor document, Scrollsheets will appear as tab-delimited tables (compatible with table generators in Windows word processors, e.g., MS Word).

The queues of Scrollsheets (and graphs).
Statistical analyses often produce large amounts of output. Scrollsheets offer flexible ways to organize the output regardless of its size. New Scrollsheets are generated by subsequent analyses in a "queue," where older Scrollsheets are closed automatically as new ones are created (to avoid too many windows).

The Scrollsheets are closed on a first-in-first-out basis, and the default length of the queue is 3. In other words, when the fourth Scrollsheet is created, then the first one is closed (with no warning unless you have edited or customized it). In some instances, you may want to increase the length of this queue (use the *Scrollsheet Manager* in the pull-down menu *Window* to change the length of the queue for the current session). Another option (*General...* in the pull-down menu *Options*) can be used to adjust the queue length permanently.

Regardless of the length of the queue, you can also "lock" individual windows (i.e., "remove" them from the queue; use the *Scrollsheet Manger* in the pull-down menu *Window*), so that they will not be automatically closed as long as you do not exit the program.

Also, as mentioned before, all Scrollsheets can be saved for a permanent record. The same queue conventions also apply to all graph windows.

Printing Scrollsheets.
Usually, in order to produce a permanent record of the output Scrollsheets, you would use the *Print* option in the pull-down menu *File* or use the shortcut method by clicking the printer icon button on the toolbar. (The shortcut method will not open the *Print Scrollsheet* options dialog but will print the entire current Scrollsheet, or a block if one was marked.)

Optional text-log of all output.
In some circumstances, however, it may be useful to automatically produce a log of all results (contents of all Scrollsheets) without having to remember about printing or saving individual Scrollsheets.

For example, at a later stage of a long sequence of tests or analyses you may want to "scroll back" and look at a result produced at the beginning of the session. In order to create such a log, select the *Automatically Print All Scrollsheets (Auto-report)* option in the *Page/Output Setup* dialog (accessible in the pull-down menu *File* or by double-clicking on the *Output* field on the status bar at the bottom of the STATISTICA window; see page 71).

In the same dialog, you will be able to specify where to direct the output: printer, a disk text-output file, and/or a scrollable *Text/output Window* (shown below).

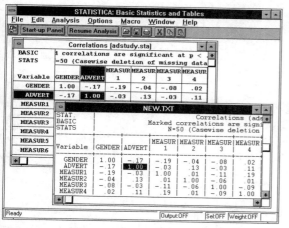

Producing graphs from a Scrollsheet. Now return to the example. While examining the Scrollsheet, you may want to view the correlations graphically. For example, visualize the correlation between variables *Measur9* and *Measur5*.

In order to produce a scatterplot for these two variables, place the cursor on the respective correlation coefficient (*-.47*) and press the right-mouse-button. In the resulting flying menu:

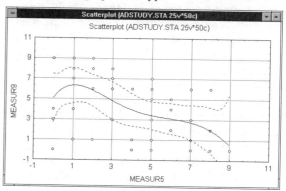

press the *Quick Stats Graphs* option, then select one of the scatterplots in the *Quick Stats Graphs* sub-menu, shown below. (See page 46 for descriptions of graphs available from the spreadsheet toolbar and flying menus.)

The requested graph will appear on the screen.

Graph customization. Note that now, when the focus is on the graph window (see above), the toolbar

has changed. The graphics toolbar (which accompanies all graph windows) looks different than the toolbars for the data spreadsheet and results Scrollsheets (which are more similar to each other). It contains a variety of graph customization and drawing tools. All of those options are also available from pull-down menus (e.g., in case you wish to record them into keyboard macros). Most of them are also available from the pop-up flying menus available by clicking on specific parts of the graph. If you click anywhere on the empty space outside the graph axes, a menu of global options will appear.

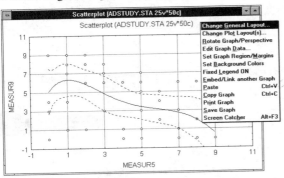

The Help system and on-line manual (*electronic manual*).
For more information on any of those options, press the help key (*F1*) when the option is highlighted or selected. STATISTICA provides comprehensive on-line documentation for all program procedures and all options available in a context-sensitive manner by pressing *F1* (there is a total of over 18 megabytes of compressed documentation included). Due to its dynamic Hypertext organization (and various facilities allowing you to customize the help system), it is usually faster to use the on-line documentation (*electronic manual*) than to look for information in the printed manuals. Help is also available by double-clicking anywhere on the help message area of the status bar on the bottom of the STATISTICA window (the status line also displays short explanations of the pull-down menu options or toolbar buttons, available when an option is highlighted or a button pressed).

Statistical Advisor. A *Statistical Advisor* facility is built into the on-line help system. When you select the *Advisor* option from the pull-down menu *Help*, the program will ask you a set of simple questions about the nature of the research problem and the type of your data, and then it will suggest to you the statistical procedures which appear most relevant (and tell you where to look for them in the STATISTICA system).

StatSoft™

ANOVA EXAMPLE

Calling the ANOVA startup panel.
In order to call the ANOVA/MANOVA module, select it from the list of all modules (statistics) in the STATISTICA *Module Switcher*.

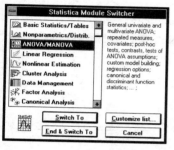

The *Switcher* can be called in a number of ways. For example, you can select the *Other Statistics* option in the pull-down menu *Analysis*. Alternatively, press the *Module Switcher* button on the toolbar (the first button on every toolbar), or simply double-click anywhere on the background of the STATISTICA window. (Note that the last method of calling the STATISTICA *Module Switcher* is analogous to calling the Windows *Task Switcher* by double-clicking anywhere on the background of the Windows desktop.)

The ANOVA module (with its startup panel) will appear.

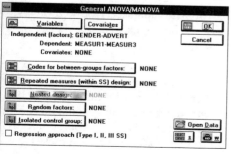

Design.
For this example of a 2 x 2 (between) x 3 (repeated measures) design, continue to use the data file *adstudy.sta*. The first (between-group) factor is *Gender* (with 2 levels: *Male* and *Female*). The second (between-group) factor is *Advert* (with 2 levels: *Pepsi* and *Coke*). The two factors are crossed, which means that there are both *Male* and *Female* subjects in the *Pepsi* and *Coke* groups. Each of those subjects responded to 3 questions (this repeated measure factor will be called *RESPONSE*: it has 3 levels represented by variables *Measur1*, *Measur2*, and *Measur3*).

Specifying the design (variables).
As usual, clicking *OK* (if variables are not selected) or pressing the *Variables* button will bring up the variable selection window. Select *Gender* and *Advert* as factors (in the *Independent variables (factors)* field) and *Measur1* through *Measur3* as dependent variables (in the *Dependent variable list* field).

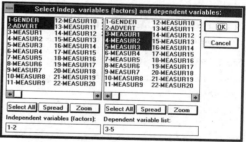

Specifying a repeated measures factor.
The minimum necessary selection is now completed and, if you did not care about selecting the repeated measures factor, you would be ready to press *OK* and see the results of the analysis. However, you need to instruct the program that the 3 dependent variables which you have selected are to be interpreted as 3 levels of a repeated measures factor. Unless you do so, the program will assume that those are 3 "different" dependent variables and would run a MANOVA (i.e., multivariate ANOVA).

In order to define the desired repeated measures factor, press the *Repeated measure (within SS) design*

button. The *Specify within-subjects (repeated measures) factors* dialog will appear.

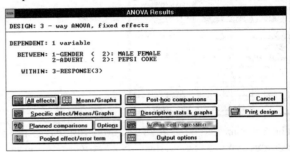

Note that the program has suggested the selection of one repeated measures factor with *3* levels (default name *RFACTOR1*), because you cannot specify more factors if only 3 variables were selected. (If, for example, you had selected 4 dependent variables, they could be used either as 4 levels of one factor or as consecutive levels of two crossed two-level factors.) You can press *F1* in this dialog to review a comprehensive discussion of repeated measures and examples of designs. You may edit the name of the factor (e.g., change the default *RFACTOR1* into *RESPONSE*), and press *OK* to exit the dialog.

Codes for between-group factors.
You do not need to manually specify codes for between-group factors (e.g., instruct the program that variable *Gender* has two levels: *1* and *2* [or *Male* and *Female*]) unless you want to prevent the program from using, by default, all codes encountered in the selected grouping variables in the data file. If you wanted to enter such custom code selection, you would press the *Codes for between group factors* button to access the *Code selection* dialog.

This dialog offers various options. For example, you can review values of individual variables before you make your selections, have the program scan the file and fill the *Codes* fields for some individual or all

variables, etc. If you do not make any entries and press *OK*, the program will automatically fill in the *Codes* fields with all distinctive values encountered in the selected variables and will close the dialog.

Performing the analysis.
When you press *OK* upon returning to the *General ANOVA/MANOVA (design specification)* dialog, the analysis will be performed and the *ANOVA Results* selection dialog will appear. You can now choose various kinds of output Scrollsheets and graphs.

Reviewing ANOVA results. Start by looking at the ANOVA summary of all effects table by clicking on the *All Effects* button (the one with a *SUMM*-ary icon).

Effect	df Effect	MS Effect	df Error	MS Error	F	p-level
1	1	8.64353	46	6.631268	1.303451	.259492
2	1	.16611	46	6.631268	.025049	.874937
3	2	40.43967	92	7.742082	5.223359	.007101
12	1	.00272	46	6.631268	.000410	.983935
13	2	2.19153	92	7.742082	.283067	.754123
23	2	5.14287	92	7.742082	.664275	.517097
123	2	4.35088	92	7.742082	.561978	.572025

Only the effect of factor number 3 (*RESPONSE*) is significant (*p=.007*) in this analysis (see the highlighted row).

Look at the marginal means for this effect to see what it means. Press the *Continue* button (either the one in the upper left corner of the current Scrollsheet or the icon-button *Continue* representing the minimized *Results* selection dialog on the bottom of the screen). When the *Results* dialog is brought back, press the

Means/Graphs button to review the means for individual effects.

This dialog contains a summary *Table of All Effects* (containing the information which you have seen before) and allows you to review individual effects from that table in the form of the plots of the respective means (or, optionally, Scrollsheets of the respective mean values).

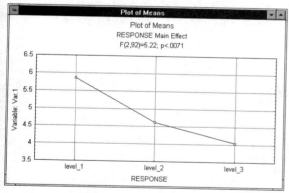

Plot of means for a main effect. Double-click on the significant main effect (the one marked with an asterisk) to see the respective plot.

The graph indicates that there is a clear decreasing trend: the means for the consecutive 3 questions are gradually lower. Even though there are no significant interactions in this design (see the *Table of All Effects*, above), look at the highest-order interaction to examine the consistency of this strong decreasing trend across the levels of the between-group factors. Press the *Continue* button (either the one in the upper left corner of the current graph or the icon *Continue*

button representing the minimized *Table of All Effects* dialog on the bottom of the screen).

Plot of means for a three-way interaction. To see the plot of the highest-order interaction, double-click on the row marked *123*, representing the interaction between factors 1 (*Gender*), 2 (*Advert*), and 3 (*Response*). An intermediate dialog will be displayed, allowing you to customize the default arrangement of factors in the graph (note that unlike the previous plot of a simple factor, the current effect can be visualized in a variety of ways). Press *OK* to accept the default arrangement.

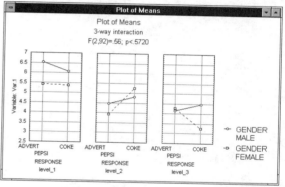

As you can see, this pattern of means (split by the levels of the between-group factors) does not indicate any salient deviations from the overall pattern revealed in the first plot (for the main effect, *Response*). Now, you can continue to interactively examine other effects, run *post-hoc* comparisons, planned comparisons, extended diagnostics, and further explore the results.

Interactive data analysis in STATISTICA. This simple example illustrates the way in which STATISTICA supports interactive data analysis: The user is not forced to specify "before seeing any results" all output to be generated. Even simple analysis designs can, obviously, produce large amounts of output and countless graphs, but usually one cannot know what will be of interest until one has a chance to review the basic output. STATISTICA allows you to select specific types of output and

StatSoft™

interactively conduct follow-up tests and run supplementary "what-if" analyses *after* the data are processed and basic output reviewed.

USER-INTERFACE IN STATISTICA (OVERVIEW)

General Features

Customized Operation

There are several ways in which the STATISTICA system can be controlled. The following sections summarize the features of the four main alternative user-interfaces of the program (interactive interface, macros, SCL command language, and control from within other Windows applications). However, note that:

- many aspects of those user-interfaces do not exclude each other, thus depending on your specific applications and preferences, you can combine them; and

- almost all features of those user interfaces represent only default settings which can be customized (leading to different appearance and behavior of the program); it is usually recommended to customize your system in order to take full advantage of STATISTICA's potential to meet your preferences and optimal requirements of the tasks which you need to accomplish (see the section on *Customizing the user-interface*, page 1).

Alternative Access to the Same Facilities; Custom Styles of Work

Even without any customization, the default settings of STATISTICA offer alternative user-interface means and solutions to achieve the same results. The "alternative access" principle present in every aspect of its user-interface allows STATISTICA to support different styles of work.

For example, most of the commonly-used tools of its interactive user-interface can be accessed alternatively from:

- traditional pull-down menus,

- via keyboard shortcuts,

- by using the toolbar ("ribbon") and the clickable fields on the status bar; and

- from the flying menus associated with specific objects (cells, graphic objects, parts of graphs) and called by clicking the right-mouse-button on the object ("context sensitive menus").

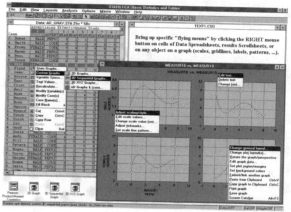

It is suggested that you explore the alternative user-interface facilities of STATISTICA before becoming "attached" to one style or another.

Interactive User-Interface

Overview

Main components of the interactive user-interface in STATISTICA. Although the interactive user-interface of STATISTICA is not the only one available (see the sections on the alternative user-interfaces, below), it is in most cases the easiest and most commonly used. The following diagram illustrates the main components of the screen (note

that usually you would not see simultaneously all of the facilities and tools shown in the diagram).

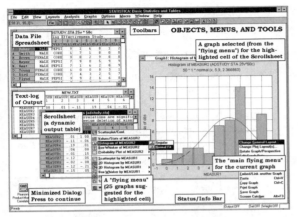

Most of the tools and facilities shown above are described in the subsequent sections of this manual (those sections are organized around the specific toolbar options accompanying each of those facilities).

Modular Structure

Modules. STATISTICA consists of modules, each containing a group of related procedures. When you switch modules, you can either keep STATISTICA down to one application window only, or alternatively, you can keep the previously used modules open, because each of them can be run in a separate window (as a separate Windows application, as described below).

When you run the modules of STATISTICA as separate applications, you will find all "general purpose" facilities (such as the data spreadsheet and all graphics procedures) available in every module and at every point of analysis.

This architecture of STATISTICA, coupled with its support for multitasking allows you not only to easily compare results from different analyses but also to run them simultaneously in different application windows.

You can quickly switch modules by:

- clicking on their icons on the desktop,

- bringing up their respective application windows (if they are already open), or

- selecting them in the STATISTICA *Module Switcher* which can be customized to facilitate quick access to the procedures you use most often.

The *Module Switcher*. The *Switcher* works in a manner similar to the Windows *Task Switcher* (which is called by double-clicking anywhere on the empty space on the Windows desktop). It can also be invoked in a similar way, by double-clicking anywhere on the empty space within the STATISTICA application window. You can also call it by pressing the first (leftmost) button on every toolbar or by selecting the option *Other Statistics* in the pull-down menu *Analysis*.

The *Module Switcher* may open new modules into the same or new application windows (see page 29, for an overview of the two ways in which the *Module Switcher* may operate).

Icons representing STATISTICA modules.
When you first install STATISTICA, *Setup* creates a group of applications on your desktop called *STATISTICA*, and sets up icons for the *Module Switcher* (see the icon *STATISTICA*, the first icon in the group, below), the *Basic Statistics and Tables* module, and some other programs (e.g., *Help*, *Setup*).

As mentioned above, you may prefer to start some modules by clicking on their respective icons on the desktop (instead of using the *Module Switcher*), thus, you may want to create icons for more modules than those automatically created by *Setup*. To create an icon for an application in a group, follow the standard Windows conventions (choose *New* in the *File* menu in *Program Manager* and create a new *Program Item*); see page 142 for a list of names of program files for all modules of STATISTICA.

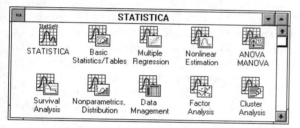

Note that when you create a new *Program Item* (icon) in a group, *Program Manager* will automatically create the respective icon for the module and label it with an abbreviated name (no wider than the icon). If you find that some of those names are not sufficiently clear, you may edit or expand the name in the *Description* field of the Windows *Program Item Properties* dialog.

Custom icon setups. You can also customize the setup of application icons by associating them with specific data files (enter the data file name into the *Command Line* field of the Windows *Program Item Properties* dialog), so that a particular data file will be open whenever you click on the module icon.

You can also create multiple icons for the same module, each associated with a different input data file (the differences may be represented by different custom names which you can assign to the icons in

their respective Windows *Program Item Properties* dialog, see the field *Description*).

The "Flow" of Interactive Analysis

Startup panel. When a module opens, a respective startup panel appears (as shown in the *Introductory Example* section, earlier).

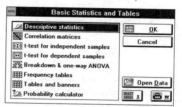

The panel provides a shortcut access to those pull-down menu facilities of the current module which the users will most likely use first. The panel saves you from having to access the menus, which usually requires additional steps. (Our tests indicate that startup panels considerably reduce the number of operations necessary in a typical STATISTICA session, especially if it involves performing a variety of analyses.) If you prefer to use the traditional interface and would rather access the pull-down menus *Analysis* or *File* (which contain all options of the startup panel), you can use them anyway because the startup panel is a modeless dialog box and clicking anywhere outside the panel will automatically iconize it (you can also suppress displaying it altogether, see page 1).

Analysis definition and output selection dialogs. When the desired analysis and (when requested) a new data file are selected in the startup panel, the analysis definition dialog will appear, where you can select the variables to be analyzed and other options and features of the task to be performed.

In some simple analyses (such as descriptive statistics, as shown on the sample screen below), the analysis definition dialog also serves as an output selection dialog where you can request the type and

StatSoft™

format of the output (e.g., some specific Scrollsheets or graphs).

Descriptive Statistics

Variables: NONE
Detailed descriptive statistics

Options
☐ Casewise (listwise) deletion of MD
☐ Display long variable names
☐ Extended precision calculations

Statistics
☐ Median & quartiles
☐ Conf. limits for means
Alpha error: 95.00 %
More statistics

OK
Cancel

Distribution
Frequency tables Histograms
☐ Normal expected frequencies
☐ K-S and Lilliefors test for normality
☐ Shapiro-Wilk's W test

Categorization
◉ Number of intervals: 10
○ Integer intervals (categories)

Box & whisker plot for all variables
Normal probability plots
Half-normal probability plots
Detrended normal probability plots
2D scatterp. /w names Matrix
3D scatterp. /w names Surface

Categorized box & whisker plots
Categorized means (interaction) plots
Categorized histograms
Categorized normal probability plots
Categorized scatterplot
3D bivariate distribution histogram

Output (queues of Scrollsheet and graph windows).

As illustrated in the two example sections above (*Introductory Example*, and *ANOVA* example), the consecutive output Scrollsheets and graphs appear in separate windows which form queues of a fixed length and are managed (i.e., automatically closed) on a first-in-first-out basis.

The default length of each of the two queues is 3. In other words, when the fourth Scrollsheet (or graph) is created, then the first one is closed. You can adjust the length of each queue (temporarily in the pull-down menu *Window* or permanently in the pull-down menu *Options*).

Regardless of the length of the queue, you can also *lock* individual windows to "remove" them from the queue (use the two *Manager* options in the pull-down menu *Window*), so that they will not close as long as you do not exit the program. Scrollsheets and graphs are managed by the same respective queues regardless of how they were produced (e.g., both Scrollsheet and graph windows can be generated automatically by the program or by you directly from spreadsheets, Scrollsheets, menus, or dialogs).

Automatic Generation of Reports and Automating Interactive Analyses

In addition to the macro- and command-based alternative user-interfaces offered in STATISTICA (see below), a variety of facilities are provided to automate conducting sequences of similar analyses and/or to automatically produce reports and printouts without having to specifically send each part of the output (Scrollsheets, graphs) to the printer or disk-output files.

Internal batch processing mode. First of all, whenever applicable, STATISTICA offers the *internal batch processing mode* option for relevant analyses. This mode is usually invoked simply by selecting not one but a list of variables to be processed. Then, the same, currently specified design or requested comparison is automatically repeated by the program for each of the selected variables (for example, the same design of multiple regression, breakdowns, *t*-test, or the Kruskal-Wallis test can be repeated for each variable in a list of dependent variables). Such procedures also offer *Internal batch processing and printing* options which will perform the requested sequence of analyses without requiring any user input and automatically send the reports to the printer or disk file.

Auto-reports and automatic printing of Scrollsheets. Regardless of whether the subsequent analyses are automatically invoked by the internal batch options (mentioned in the previous paragraph) or interactively requested by the user, you can select one of the *Auto-report* options (see the pull-down menu *Options* or the clickable *Output* field on the status bar; see page 71). These options allow you to have the contents of every output window (that will be produced in the course of subsequent analyses) sent to the printer or disk-output file without requiring any user-action.

The option to automatically produce such a record of each Scrollsheet generated on-screen is useful even if

StatSoft™

you do not intend to keep a permanent record of the output; for example, in exploratory data analyses, it is sometimes useful to be able to return to some earlier results of a long sequence of explorations. For that purpose, instead of printing, the output can be directed to a disk file, or to the temporary, scrollable *Text/output Window* (see page 67).

Automatic printing of graphs. The option to automatically print every graph that is displayed on the screen (see the clickable *Output* field on the status bar; see page 71) is mostly useful as a batch graph printing facility. In most circumstances, producing hard copies of graphs is relatively time-consuming. Thus, it is useful to use this option if you intend to print a series ("cascade") of graphs generated by a particular analysis (e.g., a long series of graphs necessary to visualize the configuration of means for a high-order interaction in ANOVA or a cascade of 3D bivariate histograms for a multi-way table). (Note that there is also a batch printing facility which can be used to print previously-saved graphs and Scrollsheets, it is available by selecting *Print Files...* from the pull-down menu *File*, see page 101.)

"Automatic pressing" of the *Continue* button to speed up the batch output. When, instead of reviewing the output on-screen, you need to quickly produce a hard copy (or a disk-output file), then it is advantageous to select the option *Auto-Exit from Scrollsheets and Graphs* (see page 103) in the *Defaults: General* dialog (option *General...* in the pull-down menu *Options*). If that option is selected, STATISTICA will "internally" press the *Continue* button on every graph and Scrollsheet, thus allowing you to print long sequences of Scrollsheets and graphs without having to press the *Continue* button at the end of every "queue-full" of documents (by default every third graph or third Scrollsheet).

Document Windows in STATISTICA

Four main types of *document windows* in STATISTICA (MDI). STATISTICA follows the standard MDI (*Multi Document User-Interface*) conventions. Each of its output windows is treated as a separate *document*, and the contents of each *document* can be managed in a variety of standard ways including editing, saving, and opening. There are four main types of documents supported in STATISTICA:

- data spreadsheets,

- output Scrollsheets,

- graphs, and

- *Text/output Windows*

(as shown in the diagram at the beginning of this section).

Integration between the *documents*. Each of the four main types of STATISTICA document-windows manages different types of "data." However, they are closely integrated not only via the optimized Clipboard support (allowing you to automatically convert one type of data into another) but also via a variety of methods to "convert" one entire document into another. For example, all text and numeric documents (or their selected subsets) can be converted into graphs in a variety of ways. Text can be incorporated into graphs, and graphs can be converted into text (i.e., numeric) representations. This architecture of STATISTICA coupled with its support for DDE (the Windows-specific data integration mechanisms) offers countless options to creatively explore the data, verify hypotheses, and present the results.

Toolbars related to active document-windows. Each of the main types of STATISTICA document-windows (see above) manages different types of data, and thus offers different customization and management options. These differences are reflected in the toolbars which accompany each type of window. Toolbar options for each of the four main types of windows are described in the respective following sections:

StatSoft™

- data spreadsheets (page 33),

- output Scrollsheets (page 44),

- graphs (page 52),

- and *Text/output Windows* (page 67).

Macros

In addition to the support for the Windows global macro recorder, STATISTICA offers an internal macro recording system which supports not only keyboard macros but also mouse actions which optionally can be played back at the speed at which they were recorded, thus they can be used to create slide-show style presentations, training materials, etc.

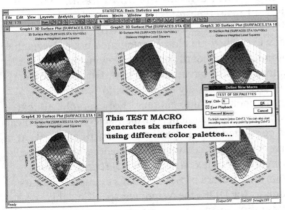

This facility (accessible at every point of your work) provides an alternative or supplement to the interactive user-interface because it allows you to specify even complex, multi-tasking macros which can then be executed repeatedly (to automate routinely-performed operations). These macros can also be used to augment the interactive user-interface; for example, a macro (initiated with a single keystroke) may contain a long variable list, case selection conditions, a repeatedly executed graph, artwork customization or an embedding operation. The macro management facilities (*Record...*, *Run...*, *Review...*) are available from the pull-down menu

Macros, or by pressing *Ctrl+F3* (for an overview of using macros, see page 74).

STATISTICA Command Language (SCL)

SCL Programs

STATISTICA can also be run in a "true" batch mode as a command-driven system using its built-in SCL (STATISTICA Command Language) application control language. You can type in sequences of plain-English commands to perform specific operations and then repeatedly execute them in batch mode. An integrated environment is provided to write and debug "batches" of SCL commands (select the Command Language option in the *Module Switcher*). The environment includes a text editor, syntax-help with examples, and a set of integrated verification facilities (see the *Options* button on the Command Language toolbar).

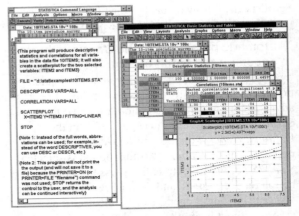

Verification facilities of the SCL editor. While writing SCL programs, you can verify not only the formal correctness of your commands, but also their consistency with the contents of the data files that are to be processed. For example, while writing an SCL program, you can verify on-line whether the requested variable names or text values exist in the specified data sets to be processed (for details, see the

on-line documentation by pressing *F1* or double-clicking on the status bar on the bottom of the window).

Interrupting execution of SCL programs.

Execution of SCL programs can be interrupted by pressing any key. STATISTICA will ask you for confirmation before the program is aborted.

Custom Extensions to SCL

Your SCL programs can include not only the predefined commands and options to perform specific statistical, data management, and graphics operations (see the toolbar *Help:Examples* and *Help:Syntax* buttons), but can also be expanded to include your own "commands" defined via the *Send Keys* facility (following the MS Excel macro language and MS Word BASIC conventions).

For example, your own extensions to SCL can perform Clipboard operations (e.g., *Copy*, *Paste*), change the default output from specific procedures, etc.

"Turn-key" Execution of SCL Programs (the STATISTICA *Run module*)

The Command Language also includes a STATISTICA *Run module* allowing you to develop "turn-key" applications which can be executed by clicking on the respective "custom application" icons on the Windows desktop.

This option is useful when the same analysis or series of analyses is executed repeatedly, and it allows your SCL programs to be used by persons unfamiliar with STATISTICA conventions.

In order to produce such a turn-key application, first write an SCL program to be executed and save it as usual (e.g., as *program1.scl*). Then use your Windows *Program Manager* to create an icon for the

application called *sta_run.exe* (this application resides in your STATISTICA directory).

STATISTICA:
Run Module

In the optional command field for the icon, specify the name of the SCL program to be executed (e.g., *d:\data\program1.scl*). Now, whenever you click on the icon, the program will be executed. You can create as many of such custom-STATISTICA-application icons as you need, and using the *Program Manager* you can assign to them meaningful names:

CLEAN AND   DAILY   BATTERY OF
VERIFY   TOTALS   OPTIMIZATION
DATA   TESTS

representing the tasks or analyses that they perform.

Controlling STATISTICA from within Other Windows Applications

Because STATISTICA supports the Microsoft Windows DDE/API interface standard, you can also build SCL (*STATISTICA Command Language*, see the previous section) commands or entire SCL scripts into macros created within and run from other Windows applications (e.g., MS Excel, MS Word, Ami Pro, Quattro Pro).

This compatibility of STATISTICA's Command Language coupled with its support of DDE for exchange of data (see page 87) and compatibility with the standard Windows file, Clipboard, and graph formats allows you to achieve a high level of integration between different Windows applications.

StatSoft™

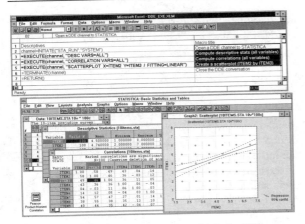

For example, an Excel macro may include SCL commands which will call STATISTICA from within Excel, perform a specified set of analyses, and then transfer and integrate specific parts of the output and/or graphs created by STATISTICA into your current Excel worksheet or workbook.

CUSTOMIZING THE OPERATION AND APPEARANCE OF STATISTICA

Customization of the User-Interface

The behavior and appearance of STATISTICA can be customized by the user and the user-interface of the program may be changed and become more elaborate as the user's needs change.

Depending on the requirements of the tasks to be performed, as well as your personal preferences for particular "modes" of work (and aesthetic choices), you can, for example:

suppress all icons, toolbars, status bars, long menus, 3D effects in tables, and request "bare-bones" sequential output with simple, paper-white Scrollsheets (output tables) and monochrome graphs, and set the system to automatically maintain no more than one simple output window at a time (see the right panel on the screen, below);

or alternatively, you could:

take full advantage of all special tools and controls, icons, toolbars, macros (e.g., assign particular tasks to specific keys), customize the output windows with colors, special fonts, and highlights, adjust the default graph styles and their display modes, extend the number of simultaneous output windows and/or *lock* "reference" graphs and Scrollsheets to create an elaborate, multilayered data analysis environment facilitating the exploration of complex data sets and allowing you to compare different aspects of the output (see the left panel on the screen, below).

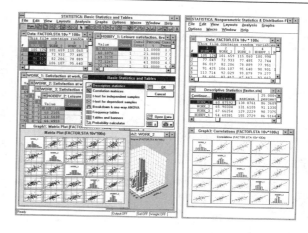

Running STATISTICA in One Application Window vs. Multiple Application Mode

One of the global system customizations of STATISTICA allows you to select whether, by default, the program will run in a single application window or as multiple applications (in their respective windows). The most immediate consequence of this setting applies to the way in which the *Module Switcher* works (see page 140): double-clicking on the name of a module in the *Switcher* will either open the new module replacing the current one, or will open a new application window for the new module without closing the previous one.

The selection of this operating mode can be made using the *Module Switching: Single Application Mode* setting, in the *Defaults: General* dialog (accessible from the pull-down menu *Options*). If the check box is marked, then STATISTICA will run in the single-application mode.

(1) Single application mode. When you select the single application window mode, then switching between modules during a STATISTICA session will not open new application windows. Each new module will be

opened into the same window replacing the module used before. Some users will like this "simple" mode because it keeps all analyses in a single application-window location and limits the number of programs opened on the desktop to a minimum.

Note that a similar effect can be achieved by pressing the *End & Switch To* button in the *Module Switcher*; the application window of the current module will close but it will not be replaced by the new one, instead, the new module will open in the "next" application window.

(2) Multiple application mode. The main advantage of the multiple application mode is that you can run different analyses (modules) simultaneously in different, simultaneously-open application windows. You can switch between the modules without closing the previous ones and take advantage of independent queues of Scrollsheets and graphs in different module application windows. This mode has clear advantages for most types of analyses allowing the user to use (and compare results of) different analytic tools.

Local vs. Permanent Customizations (Pull-down Menus *View* vs. *Options*)

Many aspects of the appearance of the program can be adjusted both in the pull-down menu *View* and *Options*.

Pull-down menu *View*. The difference between the two is that the changes requested in the pull-down menu *View* will affect the current appearance of the program (e.g., hide the toolbar) or the current document-window (e.g., change font in the spreadsheet).

Pull-down menu *Options*. Many of those options are also included in the pull-down menu *Options*

where they can be adjusted as permanent program defaults. Note, however, that those options (in the *Options* menu) which are applicable to the document-windows of a particular type (e.g., a graph or a spreadsheet) will not change that document; instead, they will only be stored as program defaults which will affect the creation of the *next* (i.e., *new*) object of the respective type.

For example, if you set the spreadsheet appearance defaults in the pull-down menu *Options*, you will see them only when you create a new file (via *New Data...* or *Import*). These defaults will not, however, affect any files opened from the disk because those files will always be brought in with the specific appearance with which they were previously saved (use the pull-down menu *View* to customize the existing objects). Typically, the defaults set for Scrollsheets and graphs will have more immediate, noticeable effects, as the program creates *new* Scrollsheets and graphs all the time.

General Default Settings and Graph Default Settings

Customization of the general system defaults. The general default settings can be adjusted at any point in the program. They control:

- the general aspects of the behavior of the program (such as maximizing STATISTICA on startup or enabling the multitasking mode),

- the way in which the output is produced (e.g., automatic printing of Scrollsheets or graphs, format of reports, buffering, etc.),

- the general appearance of the application window (icons, toolbars, etc.), and

- the appearance of document windows (colors, font),

and all of them can be adjusted in the respective dialogs accessible in the pull-down menu *Options*. Two of those dialogs are shown below.

StatSoft™

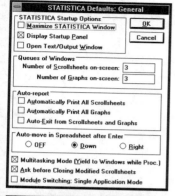

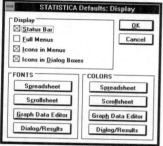

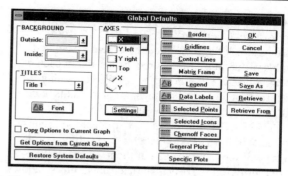

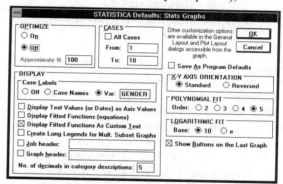

All those and other general settings are accessible regardless of the type of the document window which is currently active (e.g., a Scrollsheet or a graph).

Customization of the graphics default settings.

The graphics facilities of STATISTICA also allow you to set permanent defaults; they affect practically all aspects of the appearance of the graphs (a total of over 400 settings).

Because many of these default adjustment options are specific for particular types of graphs and they offer shortcuts to globally copy all graph settings to or from the *current* graph, the dialogs allowing you to adjust these and other graph default settings are accessible from the same pull-down menu (*Options*) only when a graph window is active.

The only exception is the dialog controlling the general conventions for accessing data by *Stats Graphs* (the option *Stats Graphs Options*),

which is always available in this menu because these options may need to be changed before any graphs are produced.

Maintaining Different Configurations of STATISTICA

STATISTICA stores all current settings and defaults in the directory from which you start the program (most of those settings are stored in a file called *statist.ini*, see the on-line documentation for more information about that file).

The fact that the configuration information is stored in the directory from which you started STATISTICA allows you to maintain different configurations of the

program for different projects or types of your work. For example, you can call STATISTICA from different disk directories, each of them associated with a different set of document files and in each of them, STATISTICA could be configured with a different set of output settings, graph defaults, etc. Alternatively, you could set up different STATISTICA icons in different application groups on the Windows desktop (each representing a project or type of job), and in each of them, specify a different *Working Directory* field (using the Windows *Program Item Properties* dialogs).

Customized Configurations for Individual Users on a Network

The same principle (see the previous paragraph) applies to network installations of STATISTICA. On a network, the program is installed in only one location (on a server disk drive), but each user can still configure the program differently because the appropriate configuration settings depend on the (local) disk drive from which the program is called. Note that you need to choose the *Network Installation* option of the STATISTICA *Setup* program in order to install it properly on a non-local drive (network server); then run the *reinst.exe* program from each workstation (to configure the workstations).

Note that a network version of STATISTICA is necessary to assure its reliable use by more than one user at a time.

StatSoft™

TOOLBARS

This section contains brief descriptions of the functions which can be requested by pressing the toolbar buttons. For a comprehensive reference on each of those functions, access the on-line *electronic manual* (press *F1* or double-click on the status bar on the bottom of the STATISTICA window) or see the program reference manuals. Note that most functions accessible through the toolbar buttons are also accessible through other controls. For example, they are accessible through the "flying menus" (which can be activated by pressing the right-mouse-button or via keyboard shortcuts) and from the pull-down menus.

Data Spreadsheet Toolbar

The spreadsheet window allows you to edit the input data and it offers a variety of data base management and data transformation/recoding operations.

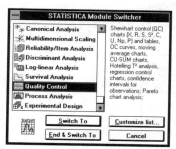

Some other specialized data management and data transformation facilities are available in the *Data Management* module. The spreadsheet toolbar provides quick access to the most-commonly used data management facilities and graphs based on raw

data. All facilities accessible via the toolbar buttons listed below are also available by using other program controls (see above).

 0. The Show Field

The *Show Field* displays the value of the currently highlighted cell at a higher precision than will fit in the respective columns of the spreadsheet. The width of the *Show Field* can be adjusted (toggled) by clicking on it with the mouse

| 3.12 | 3.1234567 | 3.12345678901237 |

or by clicking on the *Change Show* option in the pull-down menu *View*.

1. Module Switcher

Brings up the STATISTICA *Module Switcher*. The *Switcher* gives you quick access to all "modules" (i.e., groups of analytic procedures) available in your version of STATISTICA. The *Switcher* works in a manner similar to the Windows *Task Switcher* (available by double-clicking on the Windows desktop) and can be opened by double-clicking anywhere on the background of the STATISTICA window.

Depending on the current configuration, the *Switcher* may open new modules into the same or new application windows (see page 29 for an overview of the two ways in which the *Module Switcher* may operate).

Note that although the list of modules in the *Switcher* can be scrolled, it is convenient to have the modules most commonly used in your specific work listed on the top and thus not requiring scrolling; the order of modules listed can be customized by pressing the *Customize list...* button (on the *Module Switcher*).

2. Variable Specification Window (for All Variables)

Brings up the combined *Variable Specification* window; this window allows you to review/edit a table of all variable specifications (names, formats, missing data values, long labels, formulas or links, etc. defining individual variables).

Var	Name	MD Code	Format	Long Name (label, formu
7	ICE SK	-9999	8.0	"Watching ice skating"
8	HORSE R	-9999	8.0	"Watching horse racing"
9	TENNIS	-9999	8.0	"Watching tennis"
10	TRACK	-9999	8.0	"Watching track & field events"
11	SKIING	-9999	8.0	"Watching skiing competitions"
12	AUTO R	-9999	8.0	"Watching auto racing"
13	MARATHON	-9999	8.0	"Watching marathon runs"

Note that detailed variable specifications for each individual variable can be accessed by double-clicking on the variable name in the spreadsheet, which brings up a dialog containing the specifications of the selected variable.

From this individual variable specifications dialog you can also access the combined table of specifications of all variables by pressing the *All Specs* button.

3. Global Operations on Variables

Brings up a menu of global *Variable* editing/restructuring options: *Add*, *Move*, *Copy*, *Delete*, edit *Current Specs* (see page 89), edit *All Specs* (see button number 2, above), edit *Text Values* (see page 89), *Date Values* (see page 84), *Recalculate* (see page 37), *Shift (lag)*, *Rank* (see page 84), *Recode* (see page 83).

Global vs. Clipboard operations on variables. Unlike the Clipboard operations of cutting, copying, and pasting blocks of data (or contents of entire columns), these operations will affect not only the contents of the columns of data but also the columns themselves (where applicable). For example, the *Delete* operation will remove not only the contents of the selected range of columns but the columns themselves too.

Also, note the difference between these global operations performed on variables (treated as logical units of the STATISTICA data files) and all Clipboard spreadsheet operations which work the same way as in all standard spreadsheets (e.g., MS Excel).

For example, the global operation of copying, deleting, or moving variables available from this menu will not depend on the current location of the cursor or block (highlight), other than by the fact that the highlighted variable names will be suggested to you in the respective dialogs (thus offering a shortcut method of selecting variables to be affected by the

StatSoft™

operation). The operations will always be performed on all cases of selected variables, regardless of whether or not all cases or only a subset of cases are currently highlighted for the respective variables.

On the other hand, in case of Clipboard operations, only the segment of data which is highlighted will be copied, and (following the common spreadsheet conventions) pasting will always begin from the current cursor position, and proceed down.

Thus, even when you (a) highlight and copy an entire variable, (b) highlight another (entire) column and then (c) intend to paste the Clipboard content to that new location ("replacing" the previous values) -- the operation will be performed as intended only if you have placed the cursor at the top of the new column. If you placed it somewhere in the middle, then the pasting will start from that point down.

 4. Global Operations on Cases

Brings up a menu of global *Case* editing/restructuring options: *Add*, *Move*, *Copy*, *Delete*, edit/manage case *Names*.

STATISTICA: Basic						
File	Edit	View	Analysis	Graphs		
4.			Vars	Cases		
				Add...		
		Ad	Move...	g Effec		
Case		GE	Copy...	3		
			Delete...	ERT MEAS		
J. Baker		I	Names...	PSI	9
A. Smith		MALE	COKE	6
M. Brown	FEMALE	COKE	9
C. Mayer	MALE	PEPSI	7
M. West	MALE	PEPSI	7
D. Young	FEMALE	COKE	6
S. Bird	FEMALE	COKE	7
D. Flynd	MALE	PEPSI	7
J. Owen	FEMALE	PEPSI	7
H. Morrow	MALE	PEPSI	6

Global vs. Clipboard operations on cases.
Unlike the Clipboard operations of cutting, copying, and pasting blocks of data (or contents of entire rows, that is cases), these operations will affect not only the contents of the rows of data, but the rows themselves.

For example, the *Delete* operation will remove not only the contents of the selected range of rows but the

rows too (see the previous section, button 3, for more explanation and examples of the differences between the global and Clipboard operations).

 5. Text/numeric Value Display (toggle)

Toggles between displaying text values in the data spreadsheet:

Data: ADSTUDY.STA 25v * 50c								
Advertising Effectiveness Study.								
	1	2	3	4	5	6	7	8
Case	GENDER	ADVERT	MEAS	MEAS	MEAS	MEAS	MEAS	MEAS
J. Baker	MALE	PEPSI	9	1	6	8	1	2
A. Smith	MALE	COKE	6	7	1	8	0	0
M. Brown	FEMALE	COKE	9	8	2	9	8	8
C. Mayer	MALE	PEPSI	7	9	0	5	9	9

and displaying their numeric equivalents:

Data: ADSTUDY.STA 25v * 50c								
Advertising Effectiveness Study.								
	1	2	3	4	5	6	7	8
Case	GENDER	ADVERT	MEAS	MEAS	MEAS	MEAS	MEAS	MEAS
J. Baker	1	1	9	1	6	8	1	2
A. Smith	1	2	6	7	1	8	0	0
M. Brown	2	2	9	8	2	9	8	8
C. Mayer	1	1	7	9	0	5	9	9

As mentioned before (see the first section of this manual, *STATISTICA Data Files*), STATISTICA supports "double notation" of values where each value may have two "identities:" numeric (e.g., *1*) and text (e.g., *MALE*); see also *Text Value Manager*, button number 15, below, or page 89.

Note that each value may also have a long label/comment attached to it; those labels are used automatically in reports (depending on the report style setting). Those long value labels/comments can be edited and managed in the *Text Value Manager* (see page 89).

6. Case Names Display (toggle)

Toggles between displaying case names in the data spreadsheet:

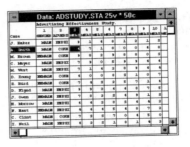

and displaying case numbers:

In order to enter, edit, or manage (e.g., change the width, copy from a variable, etc.) the current case names, double-click on any case name in the spreadsheet.

7. Zoom-in

Zooms-in (increases the font size and proportionately increases all parts of the spreadsheet).

8. Zoom-out

Zooms-out (decreases the font size and proportionately decreases all parts of the spreadsheet).

9. Increase the Column Width

Increases the width of the current column (i.e., the column marked by the current cursor position).

10. Decrease the Column Width

Decreases the width of the current column (i.e., the column marked by the current cursor position).

11. Adjust the Global Column Width

Adjusts the width of all columns of the spreadsheet (global column width adjustment).

This setting will affect the display formats of all variables in the current data file.

12. Add One Decimal

Adds one decimal place to the value display format of the current variable (for example, after pressing this button, the value *12.23* will be displayed as *12.234*).

13. Remove One Decimal

Removes one decimal place from the value display format of the current variable (for example, after pressing this button, the value *12.234* will be displayed as *12.23*).

14. Recalculate

Recalculates the current variable or, optionally, all variables defined by formulas in the current data file.

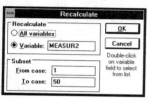

Those formulas can be entered as part of the variable specifications -- to enter/edit the specifications, double-click on the variable name in the spreadsheet or press the *Variable Specifications* toolbar button (see button number 2, above).

Note that if the intended result of the transformation is recoding of values (rather than performing arithmetic operations), there is a designated recoding facility available from the spreadsheet *Vars* button (see page 83 for details). See also page 81, for more information on data transformations in STATISTICA and on the integrated programming language Quick MML.

15. Text Value Manager

Brings up the *Text Value Manager* with all text values and long value labels/comments for the current variable.

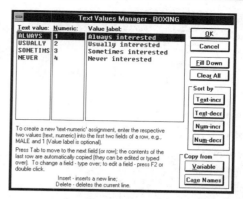

The *Manager* can be used to edit and manage (e.g., sort, copy between variables, fill, rearrange) the assignments between text and numeric values and their labels (see also page 89).

    　　16-20.
Spreadsheet Graph Buttons

The spreadsheet graphics options accessible by pressing any of the next five buttons are similar to those also available for all results Scrollsheets (see the next toolbar) except for minor differences as described in the following sections. See also the section on types of graphs in STATISTICA (page 106).

The text of the one-line data file header (displayed in the title area of the spreadsheet) is transferred to the first title field of the respective custom graphs (it can be interactively edited, customized or removed).

16. Custom 2D Graphs (from the Spreadsheet)

Brings up the *Custom 2D Graphs* definition dialog allowing you to custom-define a wide variety of 2D graphs from any combinations of cases and/or variables (or their subsets) in the current spreadsheet.

StatSoft™

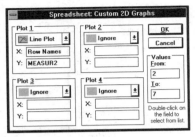

Note that not only cases and variables, but also case names and variable names can be used to define the graphs, thus not only *true-XY* (i.e., "scientific") but also simple *sequential* (i.e., "business") graphs can be defined using this facility.

Depending on the type of graph requested, case names and/or variable names are used by default to label either the axes (in true-XY graphs) or consecutive points on the axes (in sequential graphs).

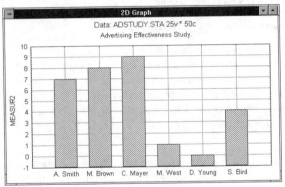

The data layout for the graph suggested by the program when the dialog appears depends on the current cursor position and/or block (highlighted) in the current spreadsheet. By default, data from the highlighted block will be plotted. (See page 106 for a summary of differences between *Custom* and *Stats* graphs in spreadsheets and Scrollsheets.)

 17. Custom 3D Sequential Graphs (from the spreadsheet)

Brings up the *Custom 3D Sequential Graphs* definition dialog allowing you to custom-define 3D sequential graphs from any combinations of rows and/or columns (or their subsets) in the current spreadsheet.

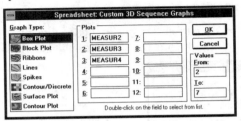

Unlike the *3D XYZ Graphs* (see the next button) where data are interpreted as triplets of *X*, *Y*, and *Z* values representing coordinates of individual observations (or units of data) in three-dimensional space, the sequential graphs provide 3D visualizations of simple sequences of values of the selected series of data (e.g., in the form of the blocks, boxes, or ribbons).

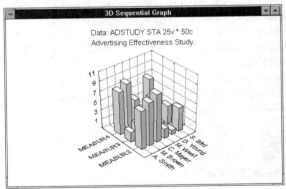

Case names or variable names (depending on whether sequences of cases or variables are plotted) are used to label the consecutive sequences of data on the Y-axis (e.g., *Measur2*, *Measur3*, *Measur4*).

 **StatSoft**™

The consecutive numbers of individual values in the plotted sequences of data (or case names) are represented on the X-axis. The actual values (represented by the "heights" of points) are plotted against the Z-axis. The data layout for the graph suggested by the program depends on the current cursor position and/or block (highlighted) in the current spreadsheet; by default, data from the highlighted block will be plotted. (See page 106 for a summary of differences between *Custom* and *Stats* graphs in spreadsheets and Scrollsheets.)

18. Custom 3D XYZ Graphs (from the spreadsheet)

Brings up the *Custom 3D XYZ Graphs* definition dialog allowing you to custom-define 3D scatterplots and surface plots from any combinations of rows and/or columns (or their subsets) in the current spreadsheet.

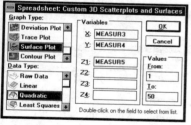

Unlike the *3D Sequential Graphs* (see the previous button) where simple sequences of data are visualized, in the 3D XYZ graphs, data are interpreted as triplets of *X, Y*, and *Z* (or multiple *Z*'s) values representing coordinates of individual observations (or units of data) in three-dimensional space. Not only cases and variables, but also case names and variable names can be used to define the X- and Y-scales (i.e., they can be defined as sequential scales). Thus, depending on the type of graph requested, case names and/or variable names are used by default to label either the (X- and/or Y-) axes or consecutive points on those axes. The Z-axis

must represent values of the plotted cases or variables.

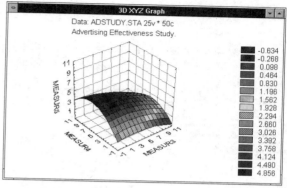

The data layout for the graph suggested by the program depends on the current cursor and/or block (highlighted) in the current spreadsheet. By default, data from the highlighted block will be plotted. (See page 106 for a summary of differences between *Custom* and *Stats* graphs in spreadsheets and Scrollsheets.)

19. Custom nD Graphs and Icons (from the spreadsheet)

Brings up the *Custom nD Graphs and Icons* definition dialog allowing you to custom-define a variety of matrix and icon graphs from any combinations of rows and/or columns (or their subsets) in the current spreadsheet.

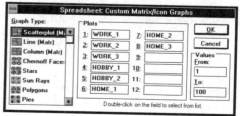

If one of the matrix plots is requested, then the selected series of data (i.e., cases or variables in the spreadsheet) are treated as "variables" in the graph

and plotted against each other (depending on the type of the graph).

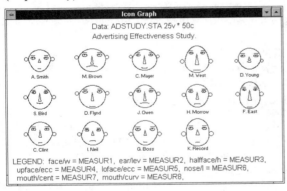

If an icon plot is requested, then the consecutive icons represent configurations of values of the cases or variables (selected for the graph) and they are labeled with the names of the consecutive cases or variables (respectively).

The data layout for the graph suggested by the program depends on the current cursor position and/or block (highlighted) in the current spreadsheet. By default, data from the highlighted block will be plotted.

(See page 106 for a summary of differences between *Custom* and *Stats* graphs in spreadsheets and Scrollsheets.)

20. Quick Stats Graphs (from the spreadsheet)

Brings up a menu of *Quick Stats Graphs* (that is, statistical graphs) for the current variable (i.e., the column where the cursor is located). Unlike *Custom Graphs* (which provide a general tool to visualize numerical output and allow you to custom-define graphs), *Quick Stats Graphs* are predefined statistical graphs. They represent either standard methods to graphically summarize raw data (e.g., various scatterplots, histograms, or plots of central tendencies such as medians) or standard graphical analytic techniques (e.g., categorized normal probability plots, detrended probability plots, or plots of confidence intervals of regression lines).

If the selected graph requires more than one variable (e.g., all categorized graphs, where the currently selected variable is plotted *across* levels of some other variable, see the next graph), a variable selection window will appear allowing you to select the missing variable.

These graphs process and represent data taking into account the currently defined case selection conditions and case weights (see the *Sel: OFF* and *Weight* fields on the status bar on the bottom of the STATISTICA window; see pages 73 and 74, respectively).

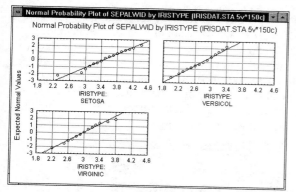

The same selection of *Quick Stats Graphs* is also accessible from all Scrollsheets, but in most Scrollsheets, the selection of variables for all bivariate *Quick Stats Graphs* is automatically determined by the program to provide meaningful visualizations of the respective results (e.g., categorized graphs).

Quick Stats Graphs vs. Stats Graphs. *Quick Stats Graphs* are easily accessible from the toolbars (as shown here) or flying menus in spreadsheets and Scrollsheets, and they include the most-commonly used types of *Stats Graphs* (*Stats Graphs* are available only from the pull-down menu *Graphs*). Although *Quick Stats Graphs* do not offer as many options as *Stats Graphs*, they are quicker to select. Unlike *Stats Graphs*:

- *Quick Stats Graphs* can be called from flying menus and toolbars (and they do not require any pull-down menu selections),

- *Quick Stats Graphs* do not require the user to select variables (the variable selection is determined by the current cursor position within a Scrollsheet or spreadsheet), and

- *Quick Stats Graphs* do not require the user to select options from intermediate dialogs (default formats of the respective graphs are produced).

21. Open Data File

Opens the file selection window allowing you to select a data file (file name extension *.sta*) and then opens the selected file in the spreadsheet window (replacing the current window).

22. Save Data File

Saves the current data file under the same or a different file name (the default data file name extension is *.sta*). If an existing file is being overwritten, then, by default, the previous file is renamed into a backup file (file name extension *.bak* instead of *.sta*).

23. Print Data File (or Highlighted Block)

Prints data from the current spreadsheet. This is a shortcut method to send the current data file to an output channel: printer, disk file, or the *Text/output Window* (depending on the current setting of the output, see the clickable *Output* field on the status bar on the bottom of the STATISTICA window, page 71).

Unlike the *Print...* (or *F4*) option available in the pull-down menu *File*, pressing this shortcut button will not open the *Print Data* options dialog (containing options to customize the format and contents of the data listing, see page 105). Instead, the entire file (or a highlighted block, if one is selected) will be sent to the output. The format of the data listing will follow the current *Print...* settings (accessible from the pull-down menu *File*). See the section on the status bar (*Output* field, page 71) for information about report styles, formatting options, adjusting margins, printing gridlines, and other output options.

StatSoft™

24. Cut (Block)

Cuts (removes) the contents of the currently highlighted cells and copies them to the Clipboard. The cleared cells are replaced with the missing data values (see page 78) of the respective variables.

Clipboard operations vs. *Global* operations on cases or variables. Note that unlike the *Global* operations performed on ranges of cases or variables and treating them as logical units (see the buttons number 3 and 4, above) the Clipboard operations follow the standard spreadsheet conventions and apply only to the contents of the selected cells. They depend entirely on the current block (highlight) and cursor position. For example, note that the *Global* operation of deleting or moving variables (see button number 3, above) will affect (remove) not only the contents of the respective columns but also the columns themselves, thus they will change the structure of the data file (and those operations will always be performed on entire variables regardless of whether all cases or only a subset of cases is currently highlighted in the selected variables). In the case of Clipboard operations, however, only the segment of data which is highlighted will be cut, and (following the common spreadsheet conventions), pasting will always begin from the current cursor position, and proceed down. Thus, for example, if in order to move a variable, you (a) highlighted and cut an entire column, (b) highlighted another (entire) column and then (c) pasted the Clipboard contents to that new location (intending to "replace" the previous values) -- the operation will be performed as intended only if have you placed the cursor at the top of the new column. If you have placed it somewhere in the middle, then the pasting will start from that point down.

25. Copy (Block)

Copies the highlighted part of the spreadsheet to the Clipboard (to select the entire spreadsheet, click on

the upper left corner of the spreadsheet). Selecting this option will copy not only the contents in the highlighted block of cells but also the case names (or numbers) and variable names associated with the highlighted cells (use *Copy Raw* from the pull-down menu *Edit* to copy only the contents of the highlighted block of cells without the corresponding case and variable names).

Data: ADSTUDY.STA 25v * 50c					
Advertising Effectiveness Study.					
	3	4	5	6	7
Case	MEASUR1	MEASUR2	MEASUR3	MEASUR4	MEASUR5
J. Baker	9	1	6	8	1
A. Smith	6	7	1	8	0
M. Brown	9	8	2	9	8
C. Mayer	7	9	0	5	9
M. West	7	1	6	2	8
D. Young	6	0	0	8	3
S. Bird	7	4	3	2	5
D. Flynd	9	9	2	6	6
J. Owen	7	8	2	3	6

Copy:

	MEASUR2	MEASUR3	MEASUR4
A. Smith	7	1	8
M. Brown	8	2	9
C. Mayer	9	0	5
M. West	1	6	2
D. Young	0	0	8
S. Bird	4	3	2

Copy Raw:

7	1	8
8	2	9
9	0	5
1	6	2
0	0	8
4	3	2

Note that blocks copied from STATISTICA spreadsheets are tab-delimited. Thus, if pasted into a word processor document, they will appear as tab-delimited tables (compatible with table generators in Windows word processors, e.g., MS Word).

Technical Note: In order to increase compatibility with other applications, STATISTICA automatically produces a variety of special Clipboard formats. For example, spreadsheet formats are produced, and will be used when you paste the contents of the Clipboard (copied from STATISTICA) into a spreadsheet document in MS Excel or Lotus for Windows.

26. Paste (Block)

Pastes the current contents of the Clipboard into the spreadsheet starting at the current cursor position. See the section on the *Cut* operation (button number 24, above) for a description of differences between *Global* operations on cases and variables (which treat them as logical units, see buttons number 3 and 4, pages 34 and 35, respectively), and Clipboard operations which follow the standard spreadsheet Clipboard conventions. For example, when you intend to copy (via the Clipboard) an entire variable to a new location, make sure that the cursor is placed at the top of the destination column, because the data will always be pasted from the cursor down (even if the entire destination column is highlighted).

Dates. In STATISTICA data files, value display formats are properties of variables and not individual cells. Therefore, if you paste into STATISTICA a block of data containing formatted date values (e.g., from MS Excel), the dates will appear as Julian (integer) values (e.g., *34092* instead of *May 3, 1993*) unless you set the format of the appropriate variables to *Date* (see page 84).

StatSoft™

Scrollsheet (Scrollable Output Window) Toolbar

Scrollsheets are "spreadsheet-like" tables used in STATISTICA to display the numeric and text output (see the *Introductory Example*, page 13). Scrollsheets can hold anywhere from a short line to megabytes of output and they offer a variety of options to facilitate reviewing the results, visualizing them in predefined and custom-defined graphs, and converting them into presentation-quality reports.

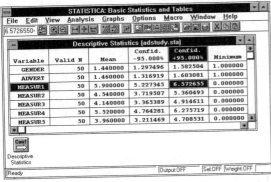

The Scrollsheet toolbar provides quick access to the most-commonly used output management facilities and graphs of the Scrollsheet data. All program control facilities that are accessible via the toolbar buttons listed below are also available from menus and via the keyboard (thus, they can be recorded into mouse-independent macros).

0. The Show Field

The *Show Field* displays the value of the currently highlighted cell at a higher precision than will fit in the current column widths.

| 1.2 | 1.234567 | 1.23456789012346 |

The width of the *Show Field* can be adjusted (toggled) by clicking on it with the mouse, or by

using the *Change Show* option in the pull-down menu *View*.

1. Module Switcher

Brings up the STATISTICA *Module Switcher* (this button is common to all toolbars, see page 140). The *Switcher* gives you quick access to all "modules" (i.e., groups of analytic procedures) available in your version of STATISTICA. Depending on the current configuration, the *Switcher* may open new modules into the same or new application windows (see page 29 for an overview of the two ways in which the *Module Switcher* may operate).

2. Zoom-in

Zooms-in (increases the font size and proportionately increases all parts of the Scrollsheet).

3. Zoom-out

Zooms-out (decreases the font size and proportionately decreases all parts of the Scrollsheet).

This option may be particularly useful to review large tables where data which meet particular criteria are marked (see button number 9, below).

 4. Increase the Column Width

Increases the column width (incrementally). Note that the column width, as well as the margin width, value display format and column names can also be adjusted in the *Scrollsheet Column Specifications* dialog. This dialog is accessible by double-clicking on the respective column name in the Scrollsheet (analogous to double-clicking on variable names in the spreadsheet).

For example, the above dialog is displayed when you double-click on the column (*Mean*) highlighted in the Scrollsheet shown in the previous section.

 5. Decrease the Column Width

Decreases the column width (incrementally, see also the previous button).

 6. Adjust Column Widths, Margins

Adjusts the column width, margin width and the width of the row name (first) column in the Scrollsheet by a specified amount of space.

The margins (which can be adjusted in this dialog) separate the active display field from the gridlines.

 7. Add One Decimal

Adds one decimal place to the value display format of the current variable (for example, after pressing this button, the value *12.23* will be displayed as *12.234*); see also button number 4, above.

 8. Remove One Decimal

Removes one decimal place from the value display format of the current variable (for example, after pressing this button, the value *12.234* will be displayed as *12.23*); see also button number 4, above.

9. Mark Cells

Marks (or un-marks) individual values or a block of values (if one is currently selected) in the Scrollsheet to make them stand out from the rest. The marked Scrollsheet values will be identified by a color other than the default data value color (by default, marked values appear red, but the color can be changed by using the pull-down menu *View*, or the *Display...* option in the pull-down menu *Options*). When printed, the marked cells will be identified with an * (asterisk) next to the value (other options to handle marked cells in printed or saved reports are available and can be selected in the *Print Scrollsheet* dialog, allowing you to customize various aspects of the Scrollsheet printing, see page 101).

StatSoft™

Cells marked by STATISTICA. Many procedures in STATISTICA automatically mark specific cells or blocks in Scrollsheets in order to "highlight" some results (e.g., unusually high frequencies in a frequency table, statistically significant correlation coefficients in a correlation matrix, or statistically significant effects in an ANOVA table of all effects).

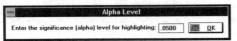

BASIC STATS	Marked correlations are significant at p < .05000 N=50 (Casewise deletion of missing data)						
Variable	GENDER	ADVERT	MEASUR 1	MEASUR 2	MEASUR 3	MEASUR 4	MEASUR 5	MEASUR 6
MEASUR6	.05	-.15	-.01	.15	.14	-.16	.23	1.00
MEASUR7	-.37	.05	-.12	.05	.04	.01	-.05	.12
MEASUR8	-.04	-.02	-.02	-.08	-.19	.01	-.19	-.33
MEASUR9	-.15	.38	-.12	-.21	.21	.10	-.47	-.27
MEASUR10	.04	.03	-.15	.05	-.09	-.24	-.07	.13
MEASUR11	-.24	.06	.18	-.21	-.02	.09	-.01	-.15
MEASUR12	-.10	-.27	.03	-.01	-.11	-.01	.11	.04
MEASUR13	-.19	.27	-.21	.14	-.14	-.12	-.03	.00
MEASUR14	.07	-.25	-.04	-.21	-.22	.14	.17	.03
MEASUR15	.02	-.05	-.08	-.00	.30	-.21	.03	.21
MEASUR16	.06	.04	-.07	.07	-.16	.11	.43	.20

Such Scrollsheets usually offer an option to change the criterion used to select the cells to be highlighted (e.g., the *p*-level for correlation coefficients) via the *Options* button on the toolbars of the Scrollsheets which are initially displayed with marked cells.

Alpha Level
Enter the significance (alpha) level for highlighting: .0500   OK

Marked values in the *Graph Data Editor*. The *Graph Data Editor* is a special type of Scrollsheet associated with each graph, which contains the specific values displayed in the graph (see page 115). In the default configuration, the values marked in that *Editor* are temporarily eliminated from the graph (this is usually done by using the interactive *Brushing* tool in the graph, see the graph toolbar button number 4, page 53). Until a marked data point is un-marked (by clicking on the *Mark values* button when the marked cell is highlighted), the point is not displayed in the graph and it is ignored when functions are fitted to the data set. This interpretation of marked values in the *Editor* can be changed by de-selecting the *Ignore Marked Values* option in the pull-down menu *View*; when that option is de-selected, then both marked and un-marked points are plotted and included in fitting.

 **10-14.**

Scrollsheet Graph Buttons

The Scrollsheet graphics options accessible by pressing any of the next five buttons are similar to those available for data spreadsheets (see the previous toolbar) except for minor differences as described in the following sections. See also the section on types of graphs in STATISTICA (page 106).

The text of the Scrollsheet titles is transferred to the title fields of the respective graphs (it can be interactively edited, customized or removed).

 10. Custom 2D Graphs (from the Scrollsheet)

Brings up the *Custom 2D Graphs* definition dialog allowing you to custom-define a wide variety of 2D graphs from any combinations of rows and/or columns (or their subsets) in the current Scrollsheet.

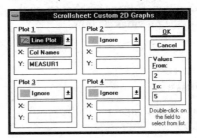

Note that not only rows and columns, but also row names and column names can be used to define the graphs, thus not only *true-XY* (i.e., "scientific") but also simple *sequential* (i.e., "business") graphs can be defined using this facility. Depending on the type of graph requested, row names and/or column names are used by default to label either the axes (in true-XY graphs) or consecutive points on the axes (in sequential graphs).

 **StatSoft**™

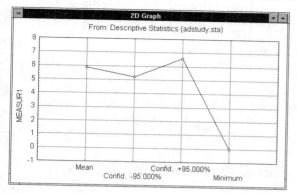

The data layout for the graph suggested by the program when the dialog appears depends on the current cursor position and/or block (highlighted) in the current Scrollsheet. By default, data from the highlighted block will be plotted. (See page 106 for a summary of differences between *Custom* and *Stats* graphs in spreadsheets and Scrollsheets.)

11. Custom 3D Sequential Graphs (from the Scrollsheet)

Brings up the *Custom 3D Sequential Graphs* definition dialog allowing you to custom-define 3D sequential graphs from any combination of rows and/or columns (or their subsets) in the current Scrollsheet.

Unlike the *3D XYZ Graphs* (see the next button) where data are interpreted as triplets of *X*, *Y*, and *Z* values representing coordinates of individual observations (or units of data) in three-dimensional space, the sequential graphs provide 3D

visualizations only of simple sequences of values of the selected series of data (e.g., in the form of blocks, boxes, or ribbons).

Scrollsheet row names or column names (depending on whether sequences of rows or cases are plotted) are used to label the consecutive sequences of data on the Y-axis. The consecutive numbers of individual values in the plotted sequences of data are represented on the X-axis. The actual values (represented by the "heights" of points) are plotted against the Z-axis.

The data layout for the graph suggested by the program depends on the current cursor position and/or block (highlighted) in the current Scrollsheet. By default, data from the highlighted block will be plotted.

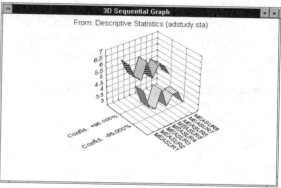

(See page 106 for a summary of differences between *Custom* and *Stats* graphs in spreadsheets and Scrollsheets.)

12. Custom 3D XYZ Graphs (from the Scrollsheet)

Brings up the *Custom 3D XYZ Graphs* definition dialog allowing you to custom-define 3D scatterplots and surface plots from any combinations of rows and/or columns (or their subsets) in the current Scrollsheet.

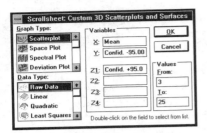

Unlike the *3D Sequential Graphs* (see the previous button) where simple sequences of data are visualized, in the 3D XYZ graphs data are interpreted as triplets of X, Y, and Z (or multiple Z's) values representing coordinates of individual observations (or units of data) in three-dimensional space. Not only rows and columns, but also row names and column names can be used to define the X- and Y-scales (i.e., they can be defined as sequential scales). Thus, depending on the type of graph requested, row names and/or column names are used by default to label either the (X- and/or Y-) axes or consecutive points on those axes. The Z-axis represents values of the plotted rows or columns.

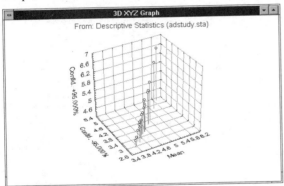

The data layout for the graph suggested by the program depends on the current cursor and/or block (highlighted) in the current Scrollsheet. By default, data from the highlighted block will be plotted. (See page 106 for a summary of differences between *Custom* and *Stats* graphs in spreadsheets and Scrollsheets.)

13. Custom nD Graphs and Icons (from the Scrollsheet)

Brings up the *Custom nD Graphs and Icons* definition dialog allowing you to custom-define a variety of matrix and icon graphs from any combination of rows and/or columns (or their subsets) in the current Scrollsheet.

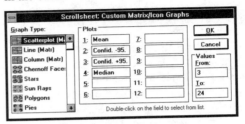

If one of the matrix plots is requested, then the selected series of data (i.e., rows or columns in the Scrollsheet) are treated as "variables" in the graph and plotted against each other (depending on the type of the graph).

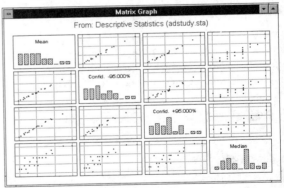

If an icon plot is requested, then the consecutive icons represent configurations of values of the rows or columns (selected for the graph) and they are labeled with the names of the consecutive rows or columns (depending on whether rows or columns are plotted).

StatSoft™

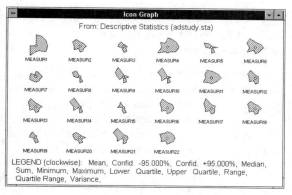

The data layout for the graph suggested by the program depends on the current cursor position and/or block (highlighted) in the current Scrollsheet; by default, data from the highlighted block will be plotted. (See page 106 for a summary of differences between *Custom* and *Stats* graphs in spreadsheets and Scrollsheets.)

 14. Quick Stats Graphs (from the Scrollsheet)

Brings up a menu of *Quick Stats Graphs* (that is, statistical graphs) for the current Scrollsheet.

Unlike *Custom Graphs* (which provide a general tool to visualize numerical output and allow you to custom-define graphs), *Quick Stats Graphs* are predefined statistical graphs. They offer either graphical methods which are specific for the type of

results displayed in the current Scrollsheet (e.g., icon plots of residuals) or they represent standard methods to graphically summarize and analyze raw data (e.g., various scatterplots, histograms, or plots of central tendencies such as medians, categorized normal probability plots, detrended probability plots). Some Scrollsheets offer non-standard graphs; in most Scrollsheets, however, the variables which will be represented in the graph (see the menu, above) depend on the current cursor position in the Scrollsheet and the type of the Scrollsheet.

For example, in descriptive statistics Scrollsheets, the variable represented by the row where the cursor is located will be suggested for graphs. For the graphs which require more than one variable (e.g., scatterplots or all categorized graphs, where the currently selected variable is plotted across levels of some other variable), the second variable will also be suggested based on the current cursor position, or the global categorical variable applicable to multiple rows and/or columns of this Scrollsheet (depending on the contents of the Scrollsheet).

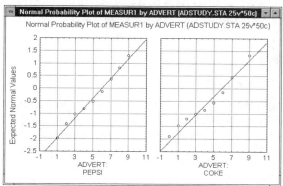

In cases when the secondary variable cannot be derived from the contents of the current Scrollsheet (or from the design of the analysis), a variable selection window will appear allowing you to select the missing variable.

Note that these graphs process and represent data taking into account the currently defined case selection conditions and case weights (see the *Sel:*

OFF and *Weight* fields on the status bar on the bottom of the STATISTICA window; see pages 73 and 74, respectively).

Quick Stats Graphs vs. Stats Graphs. *Quick Stats Graphs* are easily accessible from the toolbars (as shown here) or flying menus in spreadsheets and Scrollsheets, and they include the most-commonly used types of *Stats Graphs* (*Stats Graphs* are available only from the pull-down menu *Graphs*). Although *Quick Stats Graphs* do not offer as many options as *Stats Graphs*, they are quicker to select. Unlike *Stats Graphs*:

- *Quick Stats Graphs* can be called from flying menus and toolbars (they do not require any pull-down menu selections),

- *Quick Stats Graphs* do not require the user to select variables (the variable selection is determined by the current cursor position within a Scrollsheet or spreadsheet), and

- *Quick Stats Graphs* do not require the user to select options from intermediate dialogs (default formats of the respective graphs are produced).

 15. Open Scrollsheet File

Opens the file selection window allowing you to select a Scrollsheet file (file name extension **.scr*) and then opens the selected file in a new Scrollsheet window.

 16. Save Scrollsheet File

Saves the current Scrollsheet under the same file name (if one exists) or a new file name (the default Scrollsheet file name extension is **.scr*).

 17. Print Scrollsheet (or Highlighted Block)

Prints data from the current Scrollsheet. This is a shortcut method to send the contents of the current Scrollsheet to an output channel: printer, disk file, or the *Text/output Window* (depending on the current setting of the output, see the clickable *Output* field on the status bar on the bottom of the STATISTICA window; see page 71).

Unlike the *Print...* (or *F4*) option available in the pull-down menu *File*, pressing this shortcut button will not open the *Print Scrollsheet* options dialog (containing Scrollsheet printing options, see page 101).

Instead, the entire Scrollsheet (or a highlighted block, if one is selected) will be sent to the output channel. The format of the printout will follow the current *Print...* settings (accessible from the pull-down menu *File*).

Automatic printing. Note that if you need to keep a complete log of all Scrollsheets which are displayed on the screen without having to manually press the *Print* button for each Scrollsheet, select the *Automatically Print All Scrollsheets (Auto-report)* option in the *Page/Output Setup* dialog (accessible by double-clicking on the *Output* field on the status bar at the bottom of the STATISTICA window, see page 71).

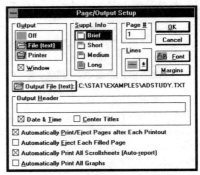

 **StatSoft**™

In the same dialog, you will be able to specify where to direct the output: printer, a disk text-output file, or a scrollable *Text/output Window*.

See the section on the status bar *Output* field (page 71) for information about report styles, formatting options, printing gridlines, adjusting margins, and other output options.

 18. Cut (Block)

Cuts (removes) the contents of the currently highlighted cells and copies them to the Clipboard.

 19. Copy (Block)

Copies the highlighted part of the Scrollsheet to the Clipboard (to select the entire Scrollsheet, click on the upper left corner of the Scrollsheet). Selecting this option will copy not only the contents in the highlighted block of cells but also the row names and column names associated with the highlighted cells (use *Copy Raw* from the pull-down menu *Edit* to copy only the contents of the highlighted block of cells without the corresponding row and column names).

Correlations [adstudy.sta]						
BASIC STATS	Marked correlations are significant at p < .05000 N=50 (Casewise deletion of missing data)					
Variable	MEASUR1	MEASUR2	MEASUR3	MEASUR4	MEASUR5	MEASUR6
MEASUR1	1.0000	.0140	-.1053	.1933	.0354	-.0137
MEASUR2	.0140	1.0000	-.0591	.0052	.0780	.1482
MEASUR3	-.1053	-.0591	1.0000	-.0891	-.2124	.1392
MEASUR4	.1933	.0052	-.0891	1.0000	.0963	-.1623
MEASUR5	.0354	.0780	-.2124	.0963	1.0000	.2276
MEASUR6	-.0137	.1482	.1392	-.1623	.2276	1.0000
MEASUR7	-.1164	.0458	.0371	.0087	-.0518	.1199
MEASUR8	-.0227	-.0842	-.1868	.0090	-.1948	-.3305
MEASUR9	-.1194	-.2142	.2062	.0953	-.4672	-.2701
MEASUR10	-.1505	.0547	-.0922	-.2374	-.0663	.1295
MEASUR11	.1836	-.2084	-.0238	.0945	-.0051	-.1497
MEASUR12	.0256	-.0101	-.1136	-.0101	.1078	.0363
MEASUR13	-.2050	.1380	-.1436	-.1171	-.0315	.0012
MEASUR14	-.0368	-.2137	-.2214	.1387	.1655	.0266
MEASUR15	-.0814	-.0015	.2973	-.2083	.0298	.2095
MEASUR16	-.0692	.0695	-.1568	.1058	.4318	.1976
MEASUR17	-.0328	.1043	.1439	.2477	-.0255	.2698

Copy:

	MEASUR2	MEASUR3	MEASUR4
MEASUR2	1.00000	-.05908	.00521
MEASUR3	-.05908	1.00000	-.08909
MEASUR4	.00521	-.08909	1.00000
MEASUR5	.07805	-.21242	.09627
MEASUR6	.14824	.13917	-.16227
MEASUR7	.04583	.03714	.00873

Copy Raw:

1.00000	-.05908	.00521
-.05908	1.00000	-.08909
.00521	-.08909	1.00000
.07805	-.21242	.09627
.14824	.13917	-.16227
.04583	.03714	.00873

Note that blocks copied from STATISTICA Scrollsheets are tab-delimited. Thus, if pasted into a word processor document, they will appear as tab-delimited tables (compatible with table generators in Windows word processors, e.g., MS Word).

Technical Note: In order to increase compatibility with other applications, STATISTICA automatically produces a variety of special Clipboard formats. For example, spreadsheet formats are produced, and will be used when you paste the contents of the Clipboard (copied from STATISTICA) into a spreadsheet document in MS Excel or Lotus for Windows.

 20. Paste (Block)

Pastes the current contents of the Clipboard into the Scrollsheet starting at the current cursor position.

Graphics Toolbar

The toolbar which accompanies the graphics window offers a selection of drawing, graph customization and multigraphics management options (e.g., linking, embedding graphs and artwork).

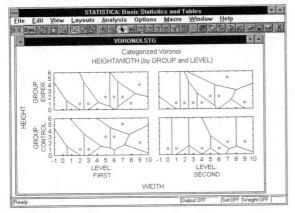

Most of the graph control and customization facilities accessible via the toolbar buttons listed below are also available from menus (thus, they can be recorded into mouse-independent macros).

0. The Show Field

The *Show Field* in the graphics toolbar displays the current coordinates of the cursor in the graph window (in spreadsheets and Scrollsheets it displays the contents of the highlighted cell, see the sections on the previous two toolbars). It acts as a "screen reader" which is dynamically updated whenever the cursor (mouse) is moved over the current (active) graph window and it displays the graph coordinate values. By default (i.e., in the *Dynamic* mode, see below), the coordinates represent the values corresponding to the X- and Y-axes of the current graph. You can switch to the *Fixed* mode by pressing

the button next to the *Show Field* (see below), and then the field will display the absolute (%) window coordinates which are independent of the graph scale: *[0, 0]%* represents the lower left corner of the window and *[100, 100]%* represents the upper right corner. The width of the *Show Field* can be toggled by clicking on it with the mouse, or by selecting the *Change Show* option on the pull-down menu *View*.

1. Dynamic/Fixed Mode (toggle)

Toggles between the *Dynamic* and *Fixed* mode for graphic object customization (see the previous paragraph for these two modes of displaying the graphics cursor coordinates).

Dynamic mode. In the *Dynamic* (default) mode, all custom objects placed anywhere on the graph (e.g., drawings, arrows, text, embedded or linked graphs or other artwork) will be anchored against the current X- and Y-axis scale coordinates.

Thus, they will be dynamically attached to specific "logical" graph locations (and not absolute positions within the graph window). When the graph is re-scaled or moved within its window, the relations between the custom (*Dynamic*) objects and the respective graph components will not change (e.g., an arrow will still mark the same point on a line graph even when the graph is re-scaled and this point is now in a different place in the window).

Fixed mode. In the *Fixed* mode, however, all custom objects will always remain in their absolute positions, anchored only against the proportions of the window.

For example, if you add a footnote at the bottom of the graph, it will always remain on the bottom even if the graph is re-scaled.

Status indicator. This button can be used as a status indicator for individual custom graphic objects -- when you highlight an object (e.g., click on a custom text label), the position of the button will reflect its status (*Dynamic* or *Fixed*).

Changing status of objects. The button can also be used to change the status of an object: after highlighting an object, press the button and the status of the object will adjust accordingly.

2. Module Switcher

Brings up the STATISTICA *Module Switcher* (this button is common to all toolbars, see page 140). The *Switcher* gives you quick access to all "modules" (i.e., groups of analytic procedures) available in your version of STATISTICA. Depending on the current configuration, the *Switcher* may open new modules into the same or new application windows (see page 29, for an overview of the two ways in which the *Module Switcher* may operate).

3. Graph Data Editor

Brings up the *Graph Data Editor* containing all data which are displayed in the current graph. In STATISTICA, all values represented in every graph can be reviewed and edited directly.

In other words, regardless of whether the graph represents raw data from the data spreadsheet, parts of a Scrollsheet output, or a set of calculated or derived scores (e.g., in a probability plot), these values are always accessible in the internal *Graph Data Editor*.

The *Editor* is organized into column-segments representing individual plots (i.e., series of data) from the current graph.

In mixed graphs, each column-segment may represent a different type of plot (e.g., line plot, scatterplot), and those types are marked by icons in the column name areas of the *Editor*. The column-segments may consist of single, double, triple or quadruple columns of values (depending on the type of the respective plot). The contents of the editor can be expanded, combined with other data, saved to a file, etc. (for more information, press *F1* in the *Editor*). When you save the graph, the complete contents of the *Editor* are also stored in the graphics file, so that later you can continue interactive data analyses (e.g., brushing, see the next button). For more information, refer to page 115.

4. Brushing Tool

Activates the *Brushing* tool; when the tool is activated, the cursor changes to a cross-hair and the program will allow you to (temporarily) mark or interactively eliminate individual data points from the graph by clicking on them with the cross-hair. A typical application for this tool is to identify outliers: When you click on a point in the graph, the point's coordinates will automatically be highlighted in the *Graph Data Editor* (see the previous paragraph), so that you can examine the data. Another application for this tool is to explore the influence of outliers on a fitted function (e.g., regression line or a polynomial fit). Clicking on a point will automatically remove it from the graph (and mark it in the *Graph Data Editor*) and re-calculate the fit.

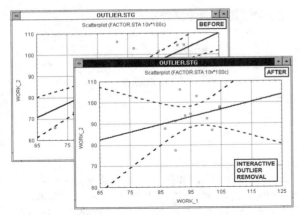

The mode of the *Brushing* tool (eliminate the point and re-plot, or only mark data points in the *Editor*) can be set using the *Ignore Marked Points* option in the pull-down menu *View*; when this option is checked, then clicking on a point in the graph will temporarily remove it. The *Brushing* tool is deactivated by clicking on the *Point Tool* (the default mode, see button number 10 below), or *Esc*.

5. Maintain Graph Aspect Ratio (*MAR* Mode)

Enables the default, *MAR* (*Maintain Aspect Ratio*) mode for graph window resizing.

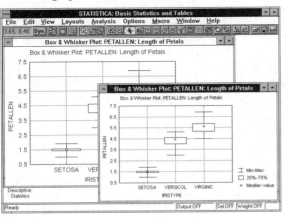

In this mode, the graph aspect ratio is maintained as you resize the window so that the graph proportions are not distorted.

By default, this button is pressed; it becomes deselected when you switch to a different mode (e.g., in order to adjust the graph proportions, see the next button). Note that after the graph proportions are modified (see the next button), pressing the *MAR* resizing button will not restore the original proportions but will allow you to automatically maintain the current graph aspect ratio when the graph window is resized.

6. Change Graph Aspect Ratio (Non-*MAR* Mode)

Enables the free (non-proportional) graph window resizing mode. In this mode, the graph can be "stretched" or "squeezed" in either direction, changing the proportions between the X and Y coordinates of 2D displays and other relations between graph components. The modified proportions of the graph will be reflected in the printout (as can be examined using the *Print Preview* facility in the pull-down menu *File*).

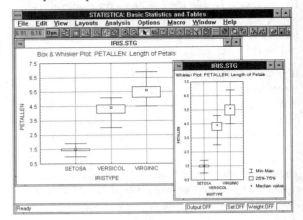

After the proportions are adjusted, you can make them permanent for this graph by switching back to the default *MAR* resizing mode (*Maintain the graph*

StatSoft™

Aspect Ratio), see the previous button; the new proportions will then be maintained.

7. Adjust Graph Area and Margins

Enables the *graph area and margins adjustment* mode. When you enter this mode, scroll-bars will appear around the graph window, allowing you to move the graph position within the graph area. However, unlike in the two previous window resizing modes (see the previous two buttons), when you resize the graph window in this mode, the graph itself will remain unaffected (i.e., its size or proportions will not change). At the same time, resizing of the window will result in adding (or subtracting) space to (or from) around the graph. This way, you can, for example, adjust the margins or add extra space on one side of the graph in order to type in or paste some text, embed or link another graph, etc.

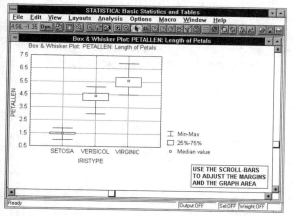

Note that in this mode, the STATISTICA application window serves as a frame of reference for all those plot area adjustment operations, thus the position of the graph window within the STATISTICA window and the relative size of the graph window will affect the available range of movement of the graph and the amount of extra space which can be added. In order to increase the space available in all directions, before you enter this mode and resize the window, place the

graph window in the middle of the STATISTICA application window and keep it no larger than about 25% of the STATISTICA application window. (See also the *Blank Graph* option in the pull-down menu *Graphs*, page 131.)

8. Zoom-in

Zooms-in (magnifies) the selected area of the graph. When you select this option (enter the *Zoom In* mode), the mouse cursor will become a "magnifier," enabling you to proportionally enlarge the current graph. Place the magnifier over the area of the graph that you want to view and click once on the left-mouse-button.

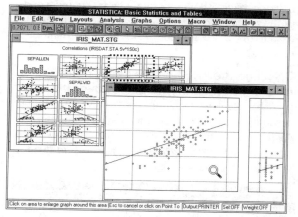

This will result in a magnified view of the specified area; the point where you click (the focal point of magnification) will become the center of the new graph window. Each time you click the mouse when you are in this mode (while the cursor looks like a magnifier), the graph area will be magnified by a factor of approximately 2; you may press it up to 5 times to achieve the magnification ratio of approximately 32:1.

Logical zoom vs. "mechanical stretching."
Note that this tool offers more than just "mechanical stretching" of the picture. Specifically, it provides a logical magnification of the selected area while

StatSoft™

maintaining the sizes of point markers, fonts, and width of all lines. Thus, the *Zoom In* tool effectively increases the "functional resolution" of the display, allowing you to inspect areas of the graph which in normal (1:1) mode were not readable due to overlapping markers or point labels. In contrast, if the zoom was "mechanical" and not logical, and the size of point markers was increased with the magnification ratio, then one would not be able to see the details (e.g., overlapping points) revealed in the illustration above.

Drawing in zoom mode. Because the *Zoom In* tool provides logical magnification (see the previous paragraph), the black editing/resizing squares (for an illustration, see *Proportional vs. nonproportional* resizing, page 59) will maintain their size independent of the zoom ratio, therefore, the zoom mode can be used to make precise modifications to free-hand drawings.

Scrolling the graph in the zoom mode (moving a "magnifying glass" over the graph). Because the zoom mode in STATISTICA is based on a *virtual plot area* technology (and not "partial redrawing"), you can use the *Zoom-In* tool in conjunction with the *graph area/margins adjusting* mode (see the previous button).

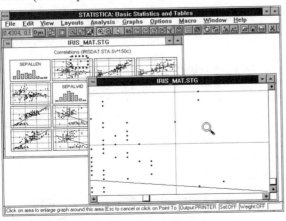

By enabling that mode, you will place scroll-bars around the graph (see above), allowing you to scroll

the magnified area in the graph window. This way of examining a graph resembles moving a "magnifying glass" over the graph.

Reversing the zoom operation. You can also decrease the graph size (in the same increments that you increased it) using the *Zoom Out* tool (see the next button). Note that unless you select exactly the same focal points for the *Zoom Out* operation as those you had used for *Zoom In*, the original location of the graph in the window will not be restored. In order to restore the original graph position (as well as the default margins and the magnification ratio) use the *Restore Defaults* option from the graph pull-down menu *View*.

 9. Zoom-out

Zooms-out (reduces the size of) the selected area of the graph. The *Zoom Out* tool works in a manner analogous to the *Zoom In* tool (see the previous button).

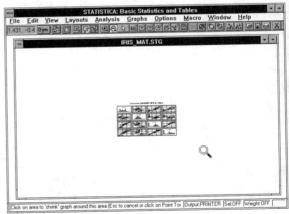

This option is useful when the details of the graph do not need to be salient but you need a lot of extra space around the graph, in order, for example, to embed some artwork or paste text for a poster or a compound graphics document. (See also the *Blank Graph* option in the pull-down menu *Graphs*, page 131.)

 **StatSoft**™

10. Point Tool (Default Mode)

Enables the *Point Tool*, which is the default mode for all graph windows (indicated when the wide button is depressed). This mode will allow you to use the left-mouse-button to select graph objects (e.g., arrows, embedded or linked objects, etc.) or different parts of the graph (e.g., titles, scales, gridlines, etc.) for customization, editing, or interactive analysis (e.g., "X-raying layers" of 3D sequential graphs). You will temporarily exit from this selection mode whenever you choose one of the interactive graph customization options (e.g., brushing, add text, draw arrows and other objects, embed graphs). Clicking on the *Point Tool* button will return STATISTICA to the default selection mode of operation.

Pressing *Esc*. Also, pressing *Esc* to exit a drawing, embedding, or brushing mode will return to this default mode. Note that the current mode (or any active graphic object manipulation operation) is always briefly referenced in the help area of the status line on the button of the STATISTICA window.

11. Graphic Text Editor

Opens the *Graphic Text Editor* -- a facility to enter, edit, and format custom text (e.g., notes, comments, or larger portions of text) in STATISTICA graphs and drawings.

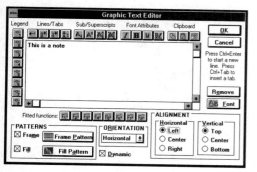

Text entered or pasted into the editor can be edited or formatted and then placed into the graph by pressing *OK* (the editor will close and the cursor will change into the editor-style cursor; move the cursor to the desired location on the graph and then click the left-mouse-button to place the text). The text can later be selected in the standard manner (by a mouse click) and moved (i.e., dragged) like every other graphic object. Double-clicking on an existing custom text will open the *Graphic Text Editor*, allowing you to edit or change the attributes of the existing text. Depending on the current status of the *Dynamic-/Fixed* switch (see page 52), the new text will be positioned on the graph dynamically (i.e., its location will adjust to all future graph changes) or in a fixed window position (e.g., always in the bottom left corner, 10% of the window width from the left). This can be changed using the *Dynamic* option in the editor (or by highlighting it and clicking on the *Dyn/Fixed* toolbar button, see page 52).

Formatting, control characters, mini-toolbar.
The *Graphic Text Editor* offers a variety of text formatting, positioning and alignment options, including multiple levels of subscripts and superscripts, legend symbols (corresponding to patterns of consecutive plots in the current graph), and many others. The simplest way to use the text attributes (e.g., italics, superscripts, etc.) is to highlight the part of text to be formatted and then press the respective button on the mini-toolbar (see below for a brief description of each of the buttons on the mini-toolbar).

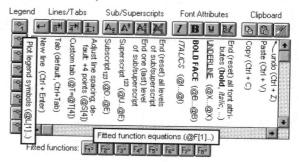

StatSoft™

STATISTICA will then insert the appropriate control characters into the text. However, you can also enter the control characters directly into the text. For example, **@B** marks the beginning and end of the bold character format (thus **@B**TEXT**@B** will appear as **TEXT**).

Control characters. The same control characters are supported in all edit fields which are used to enter graphic text in STATISTICA (e.g., titles, scale values, value labels, category names and values, legends, etc.); thus, all graphic text can be customized. Also, text customized in the *Graphic Text Editor* can be copied and then pasted into all text components of STATISTICA graphs. For more details and examples, refer to the on-line documentation by pressing *F1* in the *Graphic Text Editor* (see also page 124).

Advanced text formatting, formulas. In addition to the most-commonly used text formatting options accessible from the mini-toolbar of the *Graphic Text Editor*, a variety of advanced text formatting facilities are accessible by using the control characters (e.g., formulas can be entered and edited).

For example, custom tab stops and line spacing can be controlled in small increments; options are provided to obtain legend symbols for particular values of variables plotted in contour and surface graphs, or to automatically place in legends the values (of the plotted variable) corresponding to specific shading levels of the graph.

For more details and examples, refer to the on-line documentation by pressing *F1* in the *Graphic Text Editor*.

Combining text and graphs. Practically unlimited amounts of text can be entered (or pasted and then edited and formatted) into STATISTICA graphs, allowing you to produce documents combining text, formulas, and pictures.

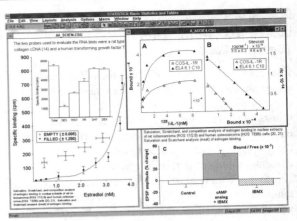

As mentioned before, you can access the *Graphic Text Editor* and customize any existing custom text in STATISTICA graphs by double-clicking on the text (left-mouse-button) or clicking on it with the right-mouse-button and then selecting the appropriate text customization operation from the flying menu which will pop up. This also applies to movable legends which have the same status as custom text (see page 121).

 12. Draw Rectangles

Enters the *rectangle drawing mode*. After pressing the button, the cursor will change into a cross-hair allowing you to draw rectangles by dragging the mouse on the graph.

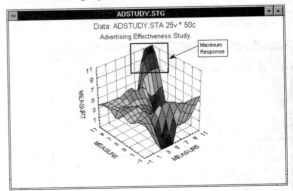

To exit from the drawing mode, click on the *Point Tool* (see the button number 10, page 57, above) or press *Esc*. The line and fill pattern depend on the current settings (as determined in the line and pattern dialogs, see buttons number 18 and 19, page 62) but can be changed later by clicking on the rectangle with the right-mouse-button and selecting the feature to be customized from the flying menu which will pop-up. Alternatively, you can later select the rectangle by clicking on it (the black selection squares will surround the rectangle), and then adjust its appearance by pressing the line or fill pattern customization buttons (see buttons number 18 and 19, pages 62 and 63, respectively).

Depending on the current status of the *Dynamic-/Fixed* switch (see page 52), each new rectangle will be positioned on the graph dynamically (i.e., its location will adjust to all graph changes) or in a fixed window position (e.g., in the bottom left corner of the window, 10% of the window width from the left).

13. Draw Rounded Rectangles

Enters the *rounded rectangle drawing mode* (see the summary on drawing and customizing rectangles, button 12, above).

14. Draw Ovals

Enters the *oval drawing mode* (see the summary on drawing and customizing rectangles, button 12, above).

15. Draw Free-hand, Polylines

Enters the *free-hand/polyline/polygon drawing mode*. After pressing the button, the cursor will change into a "brush" with a pointed tip. In order to produce free-hand drawings, press the left-mouse-button and drag the brush.

To draw a straight segment of a line, place the tip of the brush on the starting point of the segment and click the mouse, then (after releasing the button), move the tip of the brush to the endpoint of the segment, and click again. To finish drawing the object, double-click the mouse.

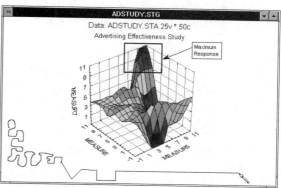

Filled shapes. Filled shapes are produced when the fill pattern is enabled (see the fill pattern customization, button number 19, page 63); note that the shape of the line or polyline does not have to be closed in order to be filled as long as it forms at least one cove (i.e., when it is not straight), as shown below.

Proportional vs. nonproportional resizing. In addition to the standard graphic object customization facilities (see the summary on drawing and customizing rectangles (button 12, above), several line-drawing specific features are supported. When the object is selected, it is surrounded by 8 (instead of the standard 4) black resizing squares. Dragging by a corner-square will allow you to proportionately-resize the drawing, whereas dragging by the middle-side-

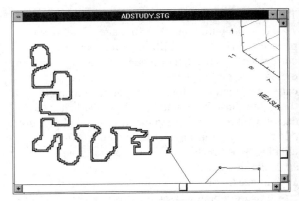

squares will allow you to resize (i.e., stretch or squeeze) the object in only one direction. The resizing mode is marked by the shape of the arrow to which the cursor will change when you move it over the resizing squares.

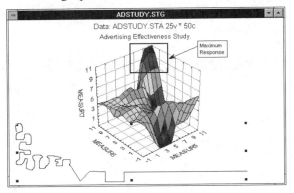

Line shape editing. Additionally, when you click again on an already-selected line drawing, you will enter the *line shape editing* mode. A black rectangle will appear in every point of the line drawing where the line changes its direction -- you can now drag any one of them with the mouse to modify the local shape of the drawing.

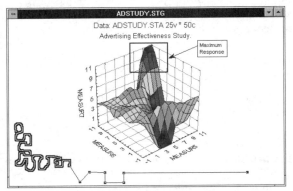

Editing in Zoom mode. True free-hand drawings will be densely covered by the squares. In order to edit such densely curved shapes, zoom-in on the drawing (see button number 8, page 55, above).

Drawings can consist of unlimited numbers of independent or overlapping segments and the order in which they will be redrawn (and, consequently, overwrite each other) can be controlled using *Redraw order control* tools (*Bring to Front* and *Send to Back*, see buttons number 20 and 21, page 63). Drawing and all other graph customization options (e.g., embedding) can be performed in every graph resizing mode, including the zoom-in mode (which can be used to increase the drawing precision, as shown in the illustration above).

 16. Draw Arrows, Custom Error Bars

Enters the *arrow and error bar drawing mode*. After pressing the button, the arrow style customization dialog will appear. A number of predefined arrow styles can be selected and countless custom arrow and error bar styles can be custom-designed using this arrow customization facility.

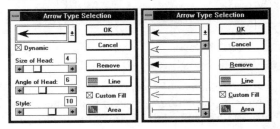

 **StatSoft**™

After pressing *OK* to accept the arrow style, move the mouse to the starting point (tail) of the arrow, then press and drag the mouse to the location where the head will be located (as if you were "pointing" in the direction of the arrow).

Adjusting the arrow position. The style as well as the precise size and location of the arrow (or the error bar) can also be adjusted later: Click on it with the right-mouse-button to select an arrow customization option from the flying menu which will pop up. To reposition an arrow, first select the arrow by clicking on it (the black resizing squares will appear on its ends); drag either of the squares to adjust the length and/or the angle of the arrow. To drag the entire arrow, place the mouse anywhere on its body (the cursor will change to the four-arrow icon) and then drag the entire object.

 17. Link or Embed Graphs and Artwork

Enters the *graph/artwork embedding or linking mode*. After pressing the button, the *Embed/Link Files* dialog will appear allowing you to specify the type of object to be incorporated in the current graph, the mode for this incorporation (*embedding* or *linking*, see the brief overview of the two modes, below), and other options for this operation.

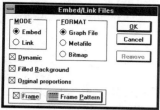

You can specify whether the foreign object will be incorporated while maintaining its original proportions, whether it will be drawn in transparent (or filled background) mode, whether it will be enclosed in a frame, etc., and if its location in the current graph will be interpreted as *dynamic* or *fixed*

(see page 52). After pressing *OK* to accept the choices, a file selection window will allow you to choose the graphics file to be accessed, and then the cursor will change into a cross-hair, as if you were drawing a rectangle. Drag the mouse to mark the new object location. As you drag, the new object-outline rectangle will either maintain the aspect ratio (of the artwork selected to be incorporated) or not, depending on whether the original object's proportions were selected in the previous dialog.

Linking vs. Embedding (overview). You can incorporate external graphics objects in STATISTICA graphs not only by pasting them (see button number 29, page 65), but also by accessing the objects directly from disk graphics files. STATISTICA supports both linked (i.e., dynamically related) and embedded (i.e., statically "built in") objects, and those objects can be accessed from graphics files in either the STATISTICA native graphics format (file name extension *.stg*), or standard Windows graphics metafiles (see page 113) and bitmaps (page 113). Note that each of the two methods of incorporating artwork from external sources into STATISTICA graphs (*linking* and *embedding*) has its advantages and disadvantages.

Linked objects. Linked objects are generally easier to modify later because instead of being actually "built into" the current graph in their entirety, they are represented in the graph only by dynamic links with their source files. Whenever the linked source file changes, the change will be

StatSoft™

reflected in the linked image of this file (which is incorporated into the current graph). Typically, the update occurs at the point of opening the compound graph document (i.e., the graph containing links to any external files). This is an advantage as compared to what it takes to modify *embedded* objects (see below), which requires at least two extra steps (see below). Specifically, whenever the source changes, embedded objects "do not know" about it because they have lost their relations with the sources; thus, they need to be manually embedded again. Also, graphics files with linked objects are more economical from the standpoint of storage space, because the external objects are in fact never duplicated: they are not part of the file. Those objects are only referenced in the current file so that the program knows where the source is located and from where it can be "read in" whenever necessary.

Embedded objects. The main advantages of using the linked graphics files--mentioned in the previous paragraph--may become their major disadvantage when you consider their portability. Specifically, graphics files with active links to other files will work properly only in the environment in which they were created. For example, when you give a copy of such a compound graph file to someone else, the links will not be updated on another computer and the linked artwork will be missing from the graph (unless the files referenced in the links are present on the other computer and reside in the same directories). Moreover, this may happen even on your own computer when you build links across the network and some drives or directories become temporarily inaccessible. To summarize, graphics files with embedded objects are larger and more cumbersome to update but at the same time they are more portable.

STATISTICA supports *embedding* and *linking* of objects across networks and it supports the Windows for Workgroups disk sharing facilities. All characteristics of the foreign objects (*linked* or

embedded) and their relation to other components of the current graph can be adjusted later by double-clicking on the embedded or linked object (or clicking on it with the right-mouse-button which will open a flying menu of available object-customization choices). The only exception is the mode for incorporating an object (*linking* or *embedding*) which can be determined only at the point of incorporating the graphics file.

 18. Adjust Line Pattern

Allows you to select the line style (pattern, color combination, size, measurement units and mode) for the currently-selected custom graphic object or (if no object is selected) for the subsequent objects which will be entered.

The line pattern customization dialog shown above is used not only for custom graphic objects but it is also common to customizations of many other line-components of STATISTICA graphs (e.g., it will appear whenever you double-click on any line or curve in any graph).

Special line customization features. In addition to the common line-customization options, this dialog offers some unique features, such as support for two-color line patterns (e.g., select any of the non-continuous line patterns, set the line to non-transparent, and choose a desired "background color" which will fill the breaks in the line pattern). The line thickness can be adjusted either in units of device-dependent pixels (and these settings will apply to pixels of any size on the screen, printer, or recorder) or in device-independent point-units (1 point = $\frac{1}{72}$ of an inch) in quarter-point increments (i.e., $\frac{1}{288}$ of an inch). Note that to achieve the desired effects when hard copies are produced, and to avoid the common

"too thin" one-pixel-wide lines printed by default on laser printers, a global minimum width for all printed lines can be adjusted in the *Print Options* dialog (see button number 26, below, see also page 137).

 19. Adjust Fill Pattern

Allows you to select the fill pattern style (pattern design, color combination, and mode) for the currently selected or (if no object is selected) for the subsequent custom graphic objects which will be entered (e.g., a rectangle, oval, or a polygon).

The pattern customization dialog shown above is used not only for custom graphic objects but it is also common to customizations of many other components of STATISTICA graphs which involve filled areas.

Special area customization features. In addition to the common area-customization options, this dialog offers some unique features, such as "transparent hatch" fill patterns or support for two-color fill patterns (e.g., set the fill-pattern to non-transparent and not solid, then choose a desired "background color" which will fill the breaks in the pattern).

 20. Bring to Front

Brings the currently selected custom graphic object to the "front." The *Bring to Front* operation allows you to place a custom graphic object "on top" of all others by changing the object redrawing order such that the current object is redrawn last and thus will remain not covered by any other objects (see also the next button, *Send to Back*).

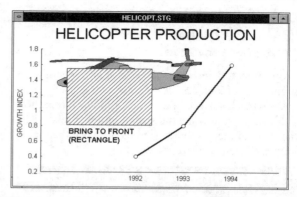

For example, if you intended to place a text on top of some artwork which was drawn (or embedded) later, you would highlight the text and press the *Bring to Front* button (alternatively, you could highlight the background object and press the *Send to Back* button, see below).

 21. Send to Back

Sends the currently-selected custom graphic object to the "back." In other words, it will be redrawn first, so that it can be covered by other custom graphic objects, which are redrawn later.

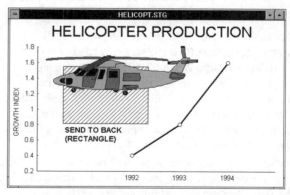

This *Send to Back* operation is analogous (i.e., opposite) to the one initiated by pressing the *Bring to Front* button (see the previous button).

 22. Global Font Size Increase

Proportionately increases the size of all fonts in the graph. This *Global Font Increase* tool is useful in cases when a small graph is to be produced (e.g., for publication) and when the size of all fonts relative to the body of the graph needs to be different than in graphs of standard size.

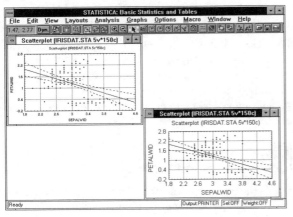

The lower graph in the screen above is the result of pressing the *Global Font Increase* button (the upper graph uses the default font).

Technical Note: *logical* **vs.** *physical* **font sizes (mapping font sizes onto plot regions of different sizes).** In STATISTICA, all graph displays and printouts can be continuously scaled along with their fonts. Unless you use the global font size adjustment facilities (as provided by the current button), the fonts will appear printed in their actual *physical* size (as set in points; 1 point = $1/72$ of an inch) if letter-size paper is used, in portrait orientation with the default (1 inch) margins on all sides, and if the default graph proportions are not modified.

The shortcut font size adjustment enabled by pressing this button allows you to effectively increase or decrease all fonts (both on the screen and in graph printouts) not by changing the specific font size

settings (e.g., not by changing a 12-point setting into a 14-point setting) but by globally adjusting the manner in which the logical font sizes are mapped into the plot region of the screen or the printout. Thus, after you press this button, a text in the graph which was set to size 10 (points) will remain set to 10, but this size (10) will now be represented by approximately 20% larger letters when displayed or printed.

 23. Global Font Size Decrease

Proportionately decreases the size of all fonts in the graph (the *Global Font Decrease* tool). This tool works in a manner analogous (i.e., opposite) to the *Global Font Increase* tool (see the previous button).

 24. Open Graph File

Opens a STATISTICA graphics file (the default file name extension is *.stg). The new graph will be opened in a separate window.

In order to access a graph or artwork in a different graphics format, use the *Link/embed* facility allowing you to access Windows graphics metafiles *.wmf or bitmap graphics files *.bmp (see button number 17, above).

 25. Save Graph File

Saves the current graph into a STATISTICA graphics file (the default graph file name extension is *.stg). The file will contain the graph with a complete set of all customizations and options, including the current set of all data displayed in the graph (as can be seen in the *Graph Data Editor*, see button number 3, above, or page 115). If an existing file is being overwritten, then STATISTICA will give you an

 **StatSoft**™

option to rename that graph file into a backup file (file name extension *.bak* instead of *.stg*).

26. Print Graph

Prints the current graph. This is a shortcut method to print the graph following the default graph printout settings (or settings as they were last modified in the *Print Options* dialog). If you need to modify any graph printout settings, use the *Print* option in the pull-down menu *File*. Unlike the *Print* button on the toolbar, using the menu option will not initiate the printing immediately, but will first display an intermediate dialog (*Print Options*) allowing you to adjust various printout and printer settings (see page 137). Use the *Print Preview* option (pull-down menu *File*) to see how the graph will appear on the page and to adjust the margins (see page 137). Note that there is also a batch printing facility available by selecting the *Print Files...* option from the pull-down menu *File*, see page 101.

27. Cut Graphic Object

Cuts (i.e., removes) the currently selected (i.e., highlighted) graphic object (such as text, label, drawing, or embedded graphs and artwork) and copies it to the Clipboard (same as *Ctrl+X*). In order to increase compatibility with other Windows applications, in addition to a copy of the object in the native STATISTICA format (see page 114), metafiles (see page 113), bitmaps (see page 113), and also text representations of the cut object are copied to the Clipboard.

28. Copy Graph, Graphic Object, or Text

Copies the entire STATISTICA graph to the Clipboard (same as *Ctrl+C*). If a graphic object (such as text, label, drawing, or an embedded graph

and artwork) is currently selected (i.e., highlighted), then only that object will be copied to the Clipboard. The same formats as in the *Cut* operation (see the previous button) are supported.

29. Paste Graph, Graphic Object, or Text

Pastes the current contents of the Clipboard into the upper left corner of the graph (same as *Ctrl+V*). You can then reposition or resize the object accordingly.

Technical Note: Pasting graphs and artwork using different graphics formats. Many applications copy objects to the Clipboard in more than one format and those formats are hierarchically organized in the Clipboard. The "top" format (the one which is used by the default Clipboard *Paste* operation) may not always be the format of your choice. The top format for all objects copied from STATISTICA applications is the STATISTICA native format (see page 114) which will typically be the most appropriate and flexible when the object is pasted back to a STATISTICA document. Thus, in those cases, the default *Paste* (*Ctrl+V*) is usually the most appropriate. However, when you paste objects from other applications, it is sometimes recommended to examine the graphics formats currently available in the Clipboard, using the *Paste Special* option in the pull-down menu *Edit*; the sub-menu of this option will list all currently available Clipboard formats allowing you to select any one of them (for pasting). Note that the Windows metafile format (see page 113) is commonly referred to as *Picture*.

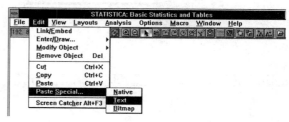

Note that *Text* pasted into STATISTICA graphs from the Clipboard can later be edited and customized in the *Graphic Text Editor* (see button number 11, above). For more information on standard Windows metafile and bitmap graphics formats, refer to page 113.

Other buttons on graphics toolbars. The following buttons appear only on toolbars for graphs which display three-dimensional representations of data.

30. Perspective and Rotation

Brings up the *Perspective and Rotation* adjustment window (see below) allowing for spinning and interactive adjustment of the point of view for three-dimensional displays.

Note that specific adjustments of the viewpoint and perspective (e.g., for an exact reproduction of a display) can also be made by editing the numeric viewpoint parameters accessible by pressing the *More Options...* button in the *General Layout* dialog (see page 118; use the pull-down menu *Layouts* or double-click on an empty area of the graph outside the axes).

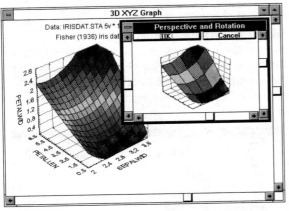

31. Animated Stratification

Initiates the *Animated Stratification* graph redrawing mode. This analytic mode, available for all 3D sequential graphs, will redraw the graph by layers ("slice by slice") pausing after displaying each "cross-section" (e.g., a layer of a surface, a ribbon, a series of range blocks or boxes) to allow you to examine the image. The process is controlled by a pop-up panel (displayed at the top of the screen, see below).

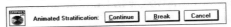

Every time you press the *Continue* button, the next "slice" is drawn. Pressing the *Break* button will complete redrawing the graph scales and labels without completing the remaining layers (e.g., allowing you to print the current cross section). Pressing the *Cancel* button will exit the animated stratification mode and redraw the entire (complete) graph.

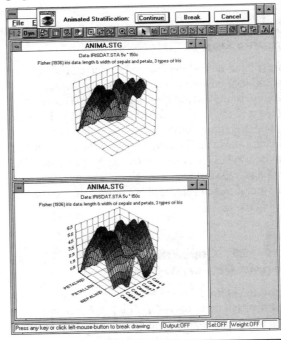

StatSoft™

Text/output Window Toolbar

The *Text/output Window* works like standard text editors (supporting block operations, search/replace, etc.) and can be used:

(1) to review/edit a log of output which was displayed in consecutive Scrollsheets in the course of analyses,

(2) to open (and review/edit) output files or any other text files; and

(3) as local notepads.

Each of those three applications is briefly described in the following paragraphs.

(1) Log of some or all Scrollsheets. In order to open a *Text/output Window* for output, check the *Text/output Window* option in the pull-down menu *View*. The window will open and then whenever you direct a spreadsheet, Scrollsheet, or a selected block of cells to the output, it will appear in the window. This output channel can also be requested in the *Page/Output Setup* dialog (accessible by double-clicking on the *Output* field on the status bar at the bottom of the STATISTICA window, or from the *Print* option in the *Options* pull-down menu, see page 71). If the *Printer* or *File* output is also selected in that dialog, the output will be directed simultaneously to the *Text/output Window* and that other channel. Alternatively, you could select the *Auto-report...* option (see page 71), and then each Scrollsheet which will be displayed on the screen will simultaneously be sent to the currently specified output channels, and thus, also to the *Text/output Window* (if one is open). See page 104 for a review of differences between the *Text/output Window* and *disk file* output.

(2) Reviewing text files. Independent of the current *Text/output Window* which was opened for output (see the previous paragraph), previously-saved text files can be opened in new text windows by choosing the *Text/output...* option in the sub-menu of the option *Open Other* (pull-down menu *File*).

(3) Notepads. Regardless of how a *Text/output Window* was opened (see the previous two paragraphs) it can always be used as a notepad (you can enter/edit text or paste it via Clipboard).

Toolbar. The *Text/output Window* toolbar provides quick access to the most-commonly used text output management facilities.

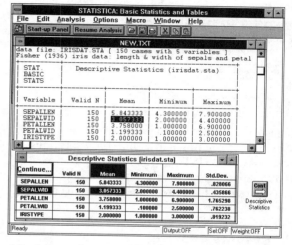

All of the options accessible via the toolbar buttons listed below are also available from menus and via the keyboard (thus, they can be recorded into mouse-independent macros).

1. Module Switcher

Brings up the STATISTICA *Module Switcher* (this button is common to all toolbars, see page 140). The *Switcher* gives you quick access to all "modules" (i.e., groups of analytic procedures) available in your version of STATISTICA. Depending on the current configuration, the *Switcher* may open new modules into the same or new application windows (see page 29, for an overview of the two ways in which the *Module Switcher* may operate).

StatSoft™

2. Startup Panel

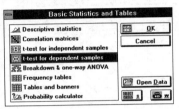

Start-up Panel

Brings up the *Startup panel* which is the first analysis selection or analysis definition dialog of the current module (the same as pressing *Ctrl+S*, or selecting the *Startup Panel* option from the pull-down menu *Analysis*).

For example, this is the startup panel of the *Basic Statistics and Tables* module.

If an analysis is already in progress, and thus by starting over you would lose some of the previous selections, STATISTICA will ask you for confirmation. Alternatively, instead of starting over, you can resume the current analysis (see the next button).

3. Resume Analysis

Resume Analysis

Resumes the current analysis by bringing to the top the last-used analysis definition or output selection window (the same as pressing *Ctrl+R*, selecting the *Resume Analysis* option from the pull-down menu *Analysis*, or pressing the floating *Cont* (continue) button).

4. Print Block

Prints the contents of the currently selected (i.e., highlighted) block of text from the *Text/output Window*.

Note that the *Text/output Window* has a different status as an output facility than spreadsheets and Scrollsheets:

One can say that the *Text/output Window* is both an on-screen "output-review tool" (like Scrollsheets) and an "output channel" (like printer or disk-output files) where you can direct output from analyses by pressing the print button.

Printing from the *Text/output Window*.

Therefore, printing from that facility is configured differently than printing from spreadsheets or Scrollsheets. When you press the *Print* button, the contents of the *Text/output Window* will be sent directly to the printer (regardless of the current setting of the *Output* field on the status bar (on the bottom of the STATISTICA window), e.g., it will be sent to the printer even if the *Printer* output is turned *Off* or directed to an output file. If you want to save the contents of the *Text/output Window* (including your notes, pasted text, etc.), use the *Save* option (see button number 6, below). If you intend to keep a complete, permanent log of all output which is displayed on the screen, the quickest way to do so is to set the *Output* to *File* (see the clickable *Output* field on the status bar on the bottom of the STATISTICA window, page 71), and in the same dialog, select the *Auto-report (Automatically Print All Scrollsheets)*. This will automatically direct the contents of all displayed output Scrollsheets to the output file. See the section on the status bar (page 71) for information about formatting options, printing gridlines, and other output options.

 ## 5. Open Text File

Opens a text file (the default file name extension is *.txt*) of your choice in the *Text/output Window*.

StatSoft™

 **6. Save
Text File**

Saves the contents of the current *Text/output Window* to a text file (the default file name extension is *.txt*); see the *Print* button (number 4, above) for more information about printing and saving the text/output files.

 **7. Cut
Block of Text**

Cuts the selected (i.e., highlighted) block of text and puts it on the Clipboard (see the next button for a note on differences between cutting from spreadsheets and Scrollsheets and the *Text/output Windows*).

 **8. Copy
Block of Text**

Copies the selected (i.e., highlighted) block of text to the Clipboard. The text copied from the *Text/output Window* is interpreted as raw, space-delimited text. Therefore, if the copied contents of the *Text/output Window* are to be used as input to be processed by another application, in most circumstances it is recommended that you copy the desired information directly from the appropriate spreadsheet or Scrollsheet (instead of the *Text/output Window*). As mentioned before, this will produce more portable, tab-delimited, or special "spreadsheet format" Clipboard representations, see the note below.

Cutting and copying from spreadsheets and Scrollsheets vs. *Text/output Windows*. Note that when you cut or copy from spreadsheets and Scrollsheets (see the first two toolbars), the contents of cells in the highlighted blocks are transferred to the Clipboard in a variety of special formats (e.g., tab-delimited, spreadsheet) which can be properly interpreted by other applications as "a set of separated values." Thus, for example, such a block pasted into

a spreadsheet applications (e.g., MS Excel, Lotus, or Quattro-Pro) will be automatically parsed into consecutive cells and not treated as undifferentiated rows of text. Also, if pasted into a word processor document, blocks copied from Scrollsheets and spreadsheets will appear as tab-delimited tables even when a proportional font is used. Also, that format is compatible with table generators in Windows word processors (e.g., MS Word). On the other hand, anything copied from the *Text/output Window* will appear in other applications as raw text, where spaces between numbers are filled with space-characters as can be seen in the window (e.g., the shorter the number, the more spaces are placed in front of it). When pasted into word processor documents, matrices of numbers formatted this way may appear out of alignment unless a non-proportional font is used.

 9. Paste Text

Pastes the text contents of the Clipboard to the *Text/output Window* starting at the current cursor location.

Status Bar (at the Bottom of the STATISTICA Window)

The status bar located on the bottom of the STATISTICA application window is used to display short help messages and explanations, and it provides quick access to some of the most-commonly used system facilities.

Progress Bar with Timer

The status bar changes into a progress bar with a timer whenever data are processed. The *Cancel* button at the end of the bar allows you to interrupt the current processing.

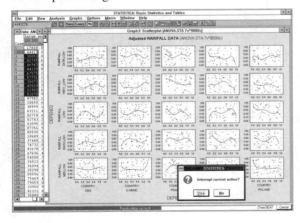

Interrupting Analyses

The timer displays the time that has elapsed from the point when the processing began. If you interrupt the

processing temporarily, the timer will continue advancing but it will automatically adjust for the length of the break if you decide to continue the processing (i.e., answer *No* to the prompt shown above).

Interrupting redraws of graphs. Note that redraws of graphs which are not accompanied by the display of the progress bar can be stopped by pressing any key or clicking with the mouse (anywhere on the screen).

Interrupting execution of SCL programs. Execution of SCL (STATISTICA command language) programs can be interrupted by pressing any key.

Multitasking

STATISTICA supports multitasking. In cases when an unusually large data set or analysis design is being processed, you can switch to another STATISTICA module (or other Windows applications) and the processing will continue in the background.

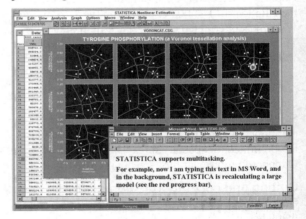

Clickable Control Fields on the Status Bar

As mentioned before, when the data are not being processed, the status bar is used to display short help messages and explanations, and it provides quick

access to some of the most-commonly used facilities which control the output (e.g., printer, output file, *Text/output Window*; report style) and the processing of data (case selection, case weights). It also displays the status of the STATISTICA macro recording or execution.

All program control facilities accessible via those status bar shortcuts are also available from menus and via keyboard (thus, they can be recorded into mouse-independent macros).

1. The Message Area

Sets the global width for the Scrollsheet columns

The Message area of the status bar, may serve as a "help button" -- when you double-click on it, the help index window will be brought up. This area is also used to display:

- Brief explanations of the currently highlighted menu choices or the toolbar buttons that are pressed, as shown above (to get a short description of a toolbar button without initiating the respective operation, keep the button pressed to read the message, then, before you release the mouse button, drag the mouse outside the button and only then release the button);

- Status information about the currently performed operation (e.g., *Extracting factors...* or *Computing residuals...*);

- Brief instructions relevant to the current stage of analysis or the operation that is being performed (e.g., when a large graph is being redrawn or updated the message reads: *Press any key or click the mouse to stop redrawing*; after pressing the *Rectangle drawing tool*, the message reads: *Drag in graph to create a rectangle (to cancel, press Esc or click the Point Tool)*).

2. Output Control

The clickable *Output: OFF* field displays the current status of the output channel (e.g., *PRINTER* instead of *OFF*). It also acts as a button: by double-clicking on it, you can access the *Page/Output Setup* dialog. This dialog is also displayed when you request output (e.g., by pressing the *Printer* button on the toolbar) at a point when no output channel (such as printer, disk file, or the on-screen *Text/output Window*) is specified. This dialog can also be accessed by selecting the *Page/Output Setup* option from the pull-down menu *File*.

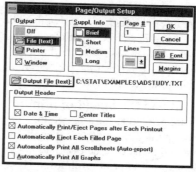

Output channel. In this dialog, you can direct the output to the *Printer*, disk *File*, and/or the optional *Window* (an on-screen text-log of output; for information on the *Text/output Window*, see the section on the *Text/output Window Toolbar*, page 67).

Report styles. You can also choose between four different *Report styles,* determining the amount of supplementary information about the current file and the selected variables that will be automatically included with the output Scrollsheets (*Brief, Short, Medium*, and *Long*; press the help button *F1* in this dialog for descriptions of the styles).

Margins. Pressing the *Margins* button opens the dialog controlling the margins of the text output.

StatSoft™

To control the paper orientation (portrait vs. landscape) for the text output, use the *Printer Setup* option from the pull-down menu *File*.

Note that the margins (as well as the page orientation, etc.) for the graphics printouts can be controlled independently (see page 120).

Other settings. You can also adjust other aspects of the printout, such as the starting page number, whether to print gridlines in the output tables (spreadsheets and Scrollsheets), and adjust the gridline style (see below), the font used, as well as the text of the optional output header to be printed on the top of each page, date, time, and centering of titles. Finally, this dialog allows you to set the page eject mode and auto-report mode (see below).

Gridlines in output and the speed of printing. Note that gridlines are printed as high-resolution graphics, thus the output is printed faster when the gridlines are suppressed (select the empty field in the list box *Lines*). If you wish to print gridlines, it is recommended to set the requested printer resolution in the *Printer Setup...* dialog for STATISTICA's text output (see pull-down menu *File*) to no more than 150 DPI (on non-Postscript printers). This will speed up printing and at the same time will not affect the quality of the output, because the fonts will still print at the highest resolution. Note also that in STATISTICA, the printer settings for text output can be adjusted independently of the printer settings for graphs (where the printer resolution setting will affect the smoothness of curves and thus you might prefer to maintain a higher-resolution default).

Automatically Print/Eject Pages after Each Printout. When this option is enabled, then after each text output is produced by the program (e.g., when requested via the *Print Data* or *Print Scrollsheet* options or the *Print* toolbar button), the

page(s) will be ejected to the printer (or output file). Thus, each printout (table) will start on a new page. If your typical output is very short (e.g., a small Scrollsheet), but you generate a lot of them, then this option may slow you down because the process of printing will be initiated very often (for each small part of output); however, the advantage of this mode is that it generates hard copies as soon as they are requested.

Automatically Eject Each Filled Page. When this option is enabled, then each page of the printout will be finalized (ejected) as soon as the page is full. This mode is somewhat slower overall, as the process of printing is initiated, separately, for each filled page. However, the advantage of this setting is that it automatically produces hard copies of the output as your analysis progresses. Alternatively, when this switch is turned off (and the *Auto Print/Eject* switch is turned off, see the previous paragraph), then all output is accumulated in an internal buffer and sent to the printer all at once at the end of the session (or whenever you select the *Print/Eject Current Pages* option in the pull-down menu *File*, which allows you to "flush out" the output buffer at any point).

Automatically Print All Scrollsheets (Auto-report). This switch allows you to automatically generate a text-log of all Scrollsheets displayed on the screen, releasing you from having to press the *Printer* button to print individual Scrollsheets. The contents of every Scrollsheet generated on the screen are automatically sent to the current output channel (printer, disk file, and/or *Text/output Window*) following the report style and conventions defined in this dialog and in the *Print Scrollsheet* options dialog (see page 101). (Note that there is also a batch printing facility which can be used to print previously-saved Scrollsheet files (file name extension *.scr) in batch, available by selecting the *Print Files...* option from the pull-down menu *File*, see page 101.)

Automatically Print All Graphs. This switch allows you to automatically generate printouts of all

StatSoft™

graphs that are displayed on the screen. The current printout setup (e.g., printer, options, margins, paper orientation, etc., as selected in the graphics window *Printer Setup* dialog) will be used. Note that there is also a batch printing facility which can be used to print previously-saved graphs (file name extension *.stg*) in batch, available by selecting the *Print Files...* option from the pull-down menu *File*, see page 101.

3. Case Selection Conditions

The clickable *Sel: OFF* field displays the current status of the *Case Selection Conditions*, that is, optional user-defined conditions (or "filters") which can be used to select a particular subset of cases for an analysis.

Normally, all cases encountered in the data file are processed (as long as they do not have missing data, see page 78). However, you may define temporary subsets of data and temporarily limit an analysis to those subsets only (e.g., only females older than 60, who either have a high cholesterol level or high blood pressure). The *Sel: OFF* field also acts as a button: by double-clicking on it, you can bring up the *Case Selection Conditions* status panel, displaying the currently-specified conditions (if any were defined).

If the conditions were accessed from a file, then information about that file is also displayed in the dialog (e.g., a comment). Unless you are at the beginning of the analysis, only the status information on *Case Selection Conditions* is displayed with no option to change them because otherwise different stages of computations would be based on different subsets of data. However, if you double-click on the status bar field at any point when the conditions can be adjusted (e.g., before an analysis is started), a different window will appear allowing you to enter or edit the text of the conditions.

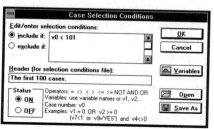

The syntax of those conditions is very simple (note the examples in the help area of the dialog).

You can refer to variables by their numbers (e.g., *v1, v2, v3, ...*; note that *v0* is the case number) or names (e.g., *income, PROFIT*). Thus, for example the condition:

Include if: `v0<101 and v1=1`

will include in the analysis only cases from the first 100 (i.e., case number has to be less than *101*) and where the value of variable number 1 (i.e., *v1*) is *1*. Note that if the name of variable number 1 was *GENDER*, and for this particular variable, *1* was equivalent to the text value *MALE* (see the section of text/numeric "double notation" of values in STATISTICA, page 89), the same case selection condition could be alternatively entered as:

Include if: `v0<101 and GENDER = 'MALE'`

The syntax of the conditions supports parentheses and various operators, and allows you to specify case selection conditions of practically unlimited complexity.

The currently-specified conditions can be preserved even if you turn off the computer (when you exit the program, STATISTICA will ask you if you want to preserve the current conditions).

Other applications for the *Case Selection Conditions*. The conditions can also be saved and used with other data sets or for different purposes in STATISTICA. The latter is possible because the same syntax and conventions are used in all facilities of the STATISTICA system which require or allow you to custom-define subsets of cases. For example, the same conventions apply to the data *Recoding* facility (available by pressing the spreadsheet button number 3, see page 34, and also page 83), data verification facilities (available in the *Data Management* module, see page 80), or all procedures which allow you to custom-define multiple subsets of data (such as frequency tables, or graphs which display multiple-subsets of data).

Case selection conditions can also be specified by pressing the *Select cases* button:

 This button is included on all startup panels and all analysis definition dialogs which are displayed before the data processing begins.

4. Case Weights

Weight:OFF

The clickable *Weight: OFF* field displays the current status of the *Case Weight* option, that is, an option to treat values of a selected variable as (integer) case multipliers when processing data. The weights can be used either for analytic purposes (e.g., some observations may be measurably more "important" and this importance can be represented by some weight scores) or to economize data storage (e.g., in some large data sets, such as some aspects of census or survey data, many cases may be identical, and thus can be represented by one case with an appropriate case weight attached to it).

The *Weight: OFF* field also acts as a button: by double-clicking on it, you can bring up the *Case Weight* status panel, displaying the weight variable (if one was defined).

Unless you are at the beginning of the analysis, only the status information on the case weight is displayed with no option to change it because otherwise different stages of computations would be based on different configurations of data. However, if you double-click on the status bar field at any point when the weight can be adjusted (e.g., before an analysis is started), a different window will appear allowing you to specify a weighting variable.:

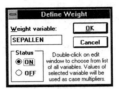

Case weights can also be specified by pressing the *case weight* button:

This button is included on all startup panels and all analysis definition dialogs which are displayed before the data processing begins.

5. Macros (Current Status)

REC

The *macro* status field (the last field of the status bar) is normally empty unless the currently performed operation involves a macro. In addition to the support for the Windows global macro recorder, STATISTICA offers an internal macro recording system which supports not only keyboard macros but also mouse actions which optionally can be played back at the same speed at which they were recorded. This allows one to design self-running "slide-shows" or educational materials (for details, see the help screens for the pull-down menu *Macros*). These

macros can also be used to augment the interactive user-interface. For example, a macro (initiated with a single keystroke) may contain a long variable list, case selection conditions, a repeatedly executed graph, artwork customization or embedding operation. When you want to start recording a macro, press *Ctrl+F3* (or select *Record...* from the pull-down menu *Macro*); the *Define New Macro* dialog will appear.

Specify the key which will be used to invoke the macro (*Ctrl* + the key) and a name under which the macro will be listed (in the *Review Macros* dialog, see the *Review...* option in the pull-down menu *Macro*). You may also set some macro recording options (see the help screen for details). When you press *OK*, the recording will begin (either including the mouse movements or not, depending on the options you have selected) and the *REC* status message will be displayed in the last field of the status bar. Note that macros which rely on any recorded mouse movements should be used only if really necessary, because in order to be played back reliably, they require that the screen arrangement is identical to the one present when the macro was originally recorded. Keyboard-based macros are much more portable between different screen environments. To stop recording, press *Ctrl+F3* again. You can play back the macro by selecting it from the *Run Macro* dialog (see the option *Run...* in the pull-down menu *Macro*).

Alternatively, you can use the keyboard shortcut assigned to the macro when it was originally recorded (i.e., *Ctrl* + the key). When a macro is being executed ("played back") the *PLAY* status message will be displayed in the last field of the status bar.

StatSoft™

QUICK REFERENCE

This section is organized in a question-and-answer format and it provides summary information on the most commonly used conventions, features, and facilities in STATISTICA.

On-line documentation (*electronic manual*).

The quickest way to obtain comprehensive information on each of the topics mentioned here (including examples and technical notes) is to use the STATISTICA *electronic manual* -- that is, the context-sensitive on-line documentation accessible by pressing *F1* or double-clicking on the status bar (on the bottom of the STATISTICA window). The on-line documentation offers Hyper-text facilities, contains a *Glossary*, and provides a complete reference to all features of the system.

Cases, Variables, Data Management

What are *cases* and *variables*?

STATISTICA data files are organized into cases and variables. If you are not familiar with this notation you can think of cases as the equivalent of records in a data base management program (or rows of a spreadsheet), and of variables as the equivalent of fields (columns of a spreadsheet). Each case consists of a set of values of variables.

	GENDER	AGE	TEST1	TEST2
case 1	male	34	12	71.4
case 2	female	35	13	66.1
case 3	female	35	12	86.1
case 4	male	28	10	88.5
case 5	female	30	14	91.0

Refer to the first section of this manual for information on the organization of data files in STATISTICA.

How to select variables for an analysis:

Every analysis definition dialog in STATISTICA contains at least one *Variables* button which allows you to specify variables to be analyzed. You can click on it (or press *V*). If you forget to specify variables and press *OK* to start the analysis, STATISTICA will ask you for the variables to be analyzed. The *Variable Selection* window which will appear supports various ways of selecting variables and it offers various shortcuts and options to review the contents of the data file (for more information and illustrations, see the *Introductory Example* section, page 13).

Can variables be selected for analyses by highlighting them in the spreadsheet?

Yes, this shortcut method is supported. If you select a block in the data spreadsheet, then the variables included in the block will automatically become pre-selected for the next analysis. Note that this shortcut is designed to limit the chance of producing unintended results because:

- The pre-selection of variables by marking a block in the spreadsheet works only as long as you have not selected a specific list of variables for the analysis (i.e., it will never overwrite your previous choices).

- Also, if the variables from the block are not what you intend to analyze, you do not need to "undo" the selection: When you enter the *Variable Selection* window, the list of pre-selected variables will be highlighted, thus, the first click of the mouse will de-select the previous range (unless you keep the *Ctrl* key pressed). If you prefer to use the keyboard to specify the list, then the first (non-cursor moving) key you press will delete the previous entry in the variable selection edit field.

How to select a subset of cases (observations) to be included in an analysis:

Before an analysis begins (i.e., before the data are processed), you can instruct the program to select only cases (i.e., rows in the spreadsheet) which meet some specific selection criteria. A facility to define and manage such *Case Selection Conditions* can be accessed from the pull-down menu *Options*, by pressing *F8*, or simply by double-clicking on the status bar field *Sel: OFF* which normally shows the current status of the *Case Selection Conditions* (when disabled, the field reads *Sel: OFF*, when enabled, the field reads *Sel: ON*). For an overview of how to use the conditions, see the section on the status bar (page 73); for a complete reference, access the on-line documentation when the *Case Selection Conditions* window is displayed.

How *Missing Data* are handled in STATISTICA:

Specifying *Missing Data* codes. A *Missing Data code*, that is, a value which signifies that there is no data for a particular case and variable (displayed as a blank cell in the spreadsheet) can be specified separately for each variable. To change the code, double-click on a variable name in the spreadsheet to access the *Variable Specifications* dialog for that variable. Alternatively, you can press the *Combined Variable Specifications* button on the spreadsheet toolbar to access a combined table for all variables (see page 34). The default *Missing Data code* in STATISTICA (used when new files are created or new variables added or data imported) is *-9999*.

Processing cases with *Missing Data*. The way in which missing data are handled when processing data can be adjusted individually for each analysis (see the field *MD deletion* in most analysis-definition dialogs). Whenever applicable, the user has the choice to eliminate them from calculations in a *casewise* or *pairwise* manner, substitute them with means, or reconstruct or interpolate them (e.g., in the

Time Series module). Press *F1* in the respective analysis-definition dialog to learn about the specific missing data handling options available for the procedures of interest.

How to add/delete variables (columns of data):

Variables may be added to and/or deleted from a data file either by (1) using the Clipboard (and optionally the *Del* key) or (2) selecting an appropriate option from the spreadsheet menu of *global* operations on variables accessible by pressing the *Vars* button on the spreadsheet toolbar.

The first method works like in regular spreadsheets and affects only the contents of columns of data but not the columns themselves. The second method adds or removes entire columns (changing the overall size of the data file). For more information on those operations, see the section on the spreadsheet toolbar (page 34).

How to add/delete cases (rows of data):

Cases may be added to and/or deleted from a data file either by (1) using the Clipboard (and optionally the *Del* key) or (2) selecting an appropriate option from the spreadsheet menu of *global* operations on cases accessible by pressing the *Cases* button on the spreadsheet toolbar.

The first method works like in regular spreadsheets and affects only the contents of rows of data but not the rows themselves. The second method adds or removes entire rows (changing the overall size of the data file). For more information on those operations, see the section on the spreadsheet toolbar (page 35).

How to split a STATISTICA data file into smaller files (how to create subfiles):

Use the *Create Subset* option from the startup panel (or the pull-down menu *Analysis*) of the *Data*

Management module. Selecting this option will bring up a dialog where you can choose not only the variables to be included in the subfile, but also *Case Selection Conditions* (see page 73).

Once your selections have been made, the current data file will be reduced to the requested subset, and you can continue the analyses using the subset of data.

Saving subsets. When you intend to save the subset, be sure to use the *Save As...* (and not the *Save*) option, unless you wish to overwrite the original (complete) data file.

Permanent vs. temporary subsets. The subset creation option is designed to be used mostly to create permanent subset files, because in order to temporarily select a subset of data to be analyzed, the on-line *Case Selection Conditions* (see page 73) are more convenient to use.

How to merge two STATISTICA data files:

A selection of data file merging procedures is available in the *Data Management* module (see the startup panel or the pull-down menu *Analysis*). Selecting this option will open a dialog of merge options. Either cases (rows of data) or variables (columns of data) can be merged. In other words, either the second file is appended to the "bottom" of the first one or it is appended to the "right side" of the first one.

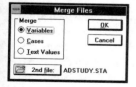

If you select to merge variables (see the first option above) then a number of additional options are available.

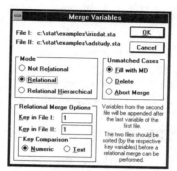

For example, you can select one of two *relational* merge options, where a key variable (in each file) is used to "match" cases based on the corresponding values of the key:

Relational **merge of variables.** When you select this mode, the cases from the second file will be matched with those of the first file, based on the values of a specified key variable.

Relational hierarchical **merge of variables.** This mode differs from the simple *relational* mode (see above) in the handling of multiple records with the same key value in either the primary or secondary file. In the simple *relational* mode (see above), successive records with identical key values will be merged. If there are uneven numbers of records with identical key values in the two files, missing data are added to "pad" the file with the lesser number of records. In contrast, in the *relational hierarchical* mode the file is padded with the values found in the last identical key record that was matched.

For more information, refer to the on-line documentation for the *Merge Variables* dialog (press *F1*).

StatSoft™

Can I merge the long value labels (or text/numeric value assignments) from two files?

Yes, when you select the *Merge files* option in the *Data Management* module (see above), in addition to the *Merge Cases* and *Merge Variables*, you will be able to choose the *Merge Text Values* option. In the subsequent dialog:

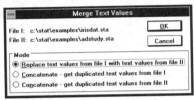

you will be able to select the way in which the text values from the two files are to be merged.

How to select (highlight) the entire spreadsheet:

Following the standard spreadsheet convention, click in the upper left corner of the spreadsheet. This shortcut is useful, for example, when you intend to copy the entire file to the Clipboard.

Note that by clicking twice in the same area, you will de-select (i.e., select and then de-select) the entire spreadsheet.

How to de-select a block in the spreadsheet:

Click twice in the upper left corner of the spreadsheet: the first click will select the entire spreadsheet, the second one will de-select it (including the block that was marked).

Alternatively, you could press *Ctrl+1* or double-click anywhere on the spreadsheet (as if you intended to edit a cell); this will de-select the block as well.

How to edit the contents of a cell (and not overwrite it):

Double-click on the cell. To avoid clearing the contents of the cell (at the point when you start entering a correction), before you start typing, first double-click on the cell. This will enter the *editing mode* and will position the cursor within the cell.

Press *F2*. Alternatively, you can follow the standard spreadsheet convention and press *F2*, which will also enter the edit mode for the currently highlighted cell.

How to verify and "clean" data:

An interactive data-verification and cleaning facility is provided in the *Data Management* module. In order to verify data, bring up the *Data Management* module, and select the option *Verify Data Values* from the startup panel or the pull-down menu *Analysis*. The *Verify Data* dialog which will appear allows you to enter the conditions to be met by the data.

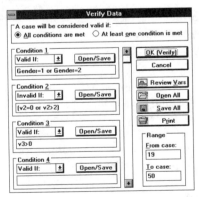

Follow the standard syntax conventions which are common in STATISTICA to all those procedures which involve any operation of "selecting cases" based on their values (see page 73). You can also use here *Case Selection Conditions* that have been previously saved to disk files (either as individual

conditions or sets). Pressing *F1* in this dialog will bring up a comprehensive description of all verification options with examples.

The verification can be as simple as checking whether values in a variable are "legal" (e.g., only *1* and *2* might be allowed for *Gender*) or whether they fall within allowed ranges of values (e.g., *Age* must be more than *0* and less than *200*). It can also be as complex as checking multiple logical conditions that some values must meet in relation to other values.

Consider the following example of conditional verification:

> *If a person is a male or less than 14 years old, then the number of pregnancies for that person cannot be more than zero.*

In order to apply these conditions, you would specify (for example):

Invalid if: `(v1='MALE' or AGE<14) and PREGN>0`

After you specify the verification conditions, press the *OK (Verify)* button and the data set (or the selected range) will be tested sequentially (one case at a time) for its consistency with the set of conditions which you have specified.

When a case is found which does not meet the conditions, then the respective row of data in the spreadsheet will be brought up and highlighted and the *Data Verification* dialog will open allowing you to either ignore the inconsistency (and continue or stop the verification) or edit (correct) the case.

For example, if you run the data verification conditions as specified on the previous *Verify Data* dialog (see above) on the example data set *adstudy.sta*, the program will detect that case number 19 does not meet condition number 3 (because in that case *v3 = 0*).

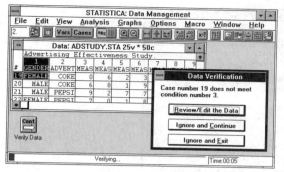

Now you can press *Review/Edit the Data* (or press *Enter*) to edit the case which is highlighted in the spreadsheet. Alternatively, you can *Ignore and Continue* or *Ignore and Exit* the verification. Note that if you decide to edit the case, then after you are done, pressing the floating *Cont* (continue) *Verify Data* button in the lower left corner of the screen will continue the verification.

How to calculate (transform) values of a variable:

Spreadsheet formulas. To perform single-line data transformation and recoding operations on single variables, you can use the data spreadsheet formulas. Double-clicking in the spreadsheet on the name of the variable which you want to transform will open the *Variable Specification* dialog (see below) where a data transformation or recoding formula can be entered directly into the *Long name (label, formula, or link)* field. Following the Windows spreadsheet formula conventions (e.g., MS Excel), start the formula with an "=" (otherwise STATISTICA will not recognize that the text is to be interpreted as a formula). For example, enter *=(v1+v2)/2*. Variables can be referenced by their names (e.g., *Income, profit, TEST1*) or numbers (e.g., *v1, v2, v3, ...*); *v0* is the case number. Logical operators can be used to define conditional transformation expressions.

StatSoft™

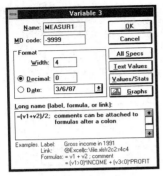

Press *F1* when you are in this dialog to access the complete on-line syntax documentation (including a list of supported functions and examples).

After entering a formula and pressing *OK*, you are given the option to recalculate the variable now. If you choose not to recalculate now, you can do so later by pressing the spreadsheet toolbar *Recalculate* button (see page 37).

The Quick MML programming language. If you need to write more complex data transformation programs than those which can be entered via spreadsheet formulas, an integrated programming language (Quick MML) can be used. The language can be accessed from the startup panel or pull-down menu *Analysis* of the *Data Management* module.

Quick MML supports loops, nested conditional statements, compound instructions, random access to individual records, custom-designed recoding functions, etc. It comes with an integrated environment that allows you to write, edit, debug, and execute your programs.

The syntax of Quick MML is very simple (it is similar to BASIC). While writing your programs, you can access *Examples* (shown in the second screen below) and a concise *Syntax* summary by pressing the respective toolbar buttons (see the *Help:Examples* and *Help:Syntax* buttons).

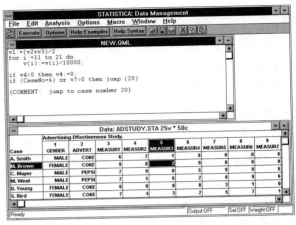

It is convenient to have the help screen available while you write your programs; you can keep the *Help* window always on top of the STATISTICA window if you set the *Always on Top* switch in the pull-down menu *Help* (in the *Help* window).

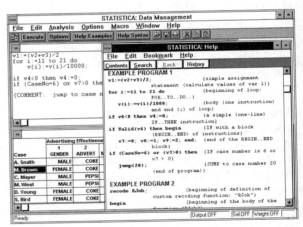

A comprehensive syntax reference with advanced examples can also be accessed by pressing *F1* (*electronic manual*).

Despite its simplicity, Quick MML is a specialized language that offers several advantages over general-purpose programming languages:

- Quick MML operates directly on STATISTICA system data files (thus, the user does not have to

be concerned about file handling, input, output, etc.); the output is written directly to the specified variables of the current data file;

- Quick MML is fully integrated into STATISTICA (e.g., it offers direct access to variable names, missing data codes, etc.) and can be run as part of a STATISTICA macro or an SCL program, etc.;

- Quick MML offers specialized procedures (not found in general-purpose programming languages) that are particularly useful for statistical data analysis and data base management (e.g., conditional deletion of cases, custom-defined data recoding functions, random sampling of cases, functions that create random variables that follow theoretical distributions, etc.).

Quick MML is well-suited for executing mathematical operations requiring very complex procedures (e.g., creating data for Monte Carlo studies) and other advanced computational operations.

What is the simplest way to recode values of a variable (e.g., split a continuous variable into categories)?

Recoding functions of practically unlimited complexity can be custom-defined in Quick MML (see above) and used repeatedly in your data transformation programs.

However, a quick on-line recoding facility can also be accessed directly from the spreadsheet at any point (see the spreadsheet toolbar button *Vars*, page 34). The scrollable *Recode Values* dialog which will be displayed allows you to define new values of the current variable (see the fields *New Value 1*, *New Value 2*, *New Value 3*, etc., below) depending on the specific conditions, which you define (see the fields *Category 1*, *Category 2*, *Category 3*, etc., below).

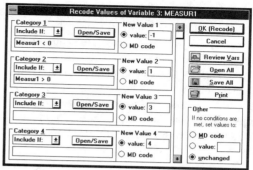

When specifying the conditions, follow the standard syntax conventions which are common in STATISTICA to all those procedures which involve any operation of "selecting cases" based on their values (see page 73). For example, the recoding conditions specified above would "translate" the negative values of the current variable (*Measur1*) into *-1* and positive values into *1*. Note that the 0's (the only value which is not included in the two recoding conditions) would be left unchanged, as set using the radio button *unchanged* (see the box *Other* in lower right corner of the dialog). You can also use here *Case Selection Conditions* that have been specified somewhere else and saved to disk files (either as individual conditions or sets). Note that recoding conditions may be much more complex (see the on-line documentation by pressing *F1* in this dialog) and they can be defined such that the new values of the current variable do not depend on the old values of that variable, but only on values of some other variables in the data set. Thus, this facility can be used not only to recode existing data, but also to create values of a new variable based on conditions met by other variables (as illustrated in the next topic).

How to create values of a new variable based on conditions met by other variables:

You can use any of the data transformation facilities: spreadsheet formulas or Quick MML (see page 81).

However, often the quickest way to do it would be to use the on-line data recoding facility described in the previous paragraph, which is accessible at any point from the data spreadsheet (see the spreadsheet toolbar button *Vars*, page 34). As mentioned in the previous paragraph, the currently highlighted variable does not even have to be included in the text of the recoding conditions. Thus, you can use this facility to create values of a variable based on conditions met by other variables.

For example, you can add a new (empty) variable to the data file, and then use this facility to create the new values. For instance, the recoding conditions could be used to assign *1*'s to the new variable for all "male subjects, 18 to 25 years old with cholesterol levels below 200;" *2*'s -- to "male subjects 18 to 25 years old with cholesterol levels above 200;" and assign the missing data value to all other subjects.

How to rank-order values of a variable (replace values with their ranks):

Select the *Rank* option by pressing the *Vars* (*variables*) button on the spreadsheet toolbar (see page 34) to bring up the *Rank Variables* dialog.

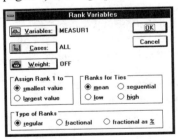

Then press the *Variables* button to select the variables to be ranked. Optionally, you can also specify a subset of cases to be affected by the operation (*Cases*, see page 73), use case weights (*Weight*, see page 74), and set a number of options to perform particular (non-default) types of ranking

(press *F1* in this dialog to access the on-line documentation).

How are *dates* represented in STATISTICA data files?

Date values of variables are internally stored in Julian format (i.e., as a single integer value that represents the number of days that have passed since January 1, 1900; for example a date entered and displayed as *1/21/1968* will be stored as the Julian date *24858*). Date values stored in this manner can be used in subsequent analyses (e.g., in *Survival Analysis* in order to calculate survival times, see below) and transformed using arithmetic operations; at the same time, they can be displayed as dates in reports or graphs (e.g., used to label scale values).

Julian date values can be displayed in the spreadsheet in numeric (Julian) format or in one of several pre-defined date display formats (e.g., *1/6/64, 6-Jan-64, Jan-1964, 01/06/64, 01/06/1964, 6-Jan*). To change the date display format, select the *Date* format option in the *Current Specs* dialog (accessible by double-clicking on the variable name in the spreadsheet or from the spreadsheet *Edit* pull-down menu) and choose one of the pre-defined display formats from the combo box.

When entering dates into a new variable, you will first need to change the variable display format from *Decimal* (the default format) to *Date* in the *Current Specs* dialog and select the desired date display

format. Now, you can enter the dates in any of the pre-defined date display formats (i.e., enter the dates in the format that is easiest to key in, even if it is different than the desired display format) and STATISTICA will recognize those formats, convert the display to the desired date format, and internally store the date values in Julian format. Please refer to the on-line *electronic manual* for more detailed information on entering new or pasting copied date values into the data file.

You can create a single date variable from two (month, year or day, month) or three (day, month, year) variables as well as split a single date variable into two or three variables in the *Date Operations* dialog accessible from the *Date Values* option in the spreadsheet *Vars* pull-down menu (see below).

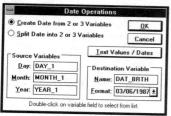

Please refer to the on-line *electronic manual* (click *F1* in the dialog shown above) for examples of creating date variables from numeric variables and splitting date variables into numeric variables.

How to use *date-*values as codes (e.g., as values of grouping variables):

Most procedures in STATISTICA require that values of grouping variables (codes) be less than 32,000, i.e., less than the Julian values of some dates. In order to use date values as codes, convert them into text values using the facility described in the next topic.

How to convert *date-*values into text values and vice-versa:

In some circumstances it may be useful to create text values with date information (e.g., when using a date variable as a coding variable). In this case, you can transform the date variable into a variable containing date text values with numeric equivalents in a range that will allow STATISTICA to use them as codes (i.e., numeric values less than 32,000), in the *Text Values/Dates* dialog.

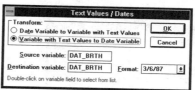

This dialog is accessible by pressing the *Text Values/Dates* button in the *Date Operations* dialog (see the previous topic).

How to restore an inadvertently overwritten data file:

When you are overwriting an existing data file (while performing the *Save As...* operation), STATISTICA will give you an option to create a backup (under the same file name but with the file name extension **.bak*). As long as you do not use *Save As...* twice in a row (which will overwrite the backup), you can return to the file as it was before being saved by using the backup.

How to perform a multiple sort:

Use the *Sort* option from the startup panel (or the pull-down menu *Analysis*) of the *Data Management* module. This will bring up a dialog where you can specify the key variables and the type of sort.

StatSoft™

If you need to sort based on more than 3 keys, press the *More Keys...* button to switch to a larger dialog.

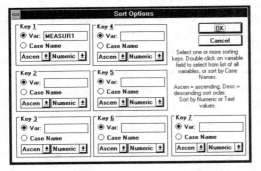

How to transpose data (convert cases into variables):

Use the *Transpose* option accessible from the data spreadsheet *Edit* menu. A hierarchical menu will allow you to select either the *Block* or *Data file* transposing option.

Transposing a block of data. The block transposing operation will affect only the contents of cells in the currently selected block highlighted in the data spreadsheet (the block must be square); the variable names and case names will not be affected. For example, the *Transpose Block* command executed on the following square block of data:

will produce the following result:

Transposing a data file. The data file transposing option will restructure the entire file. For example, transposing the data file shown above (before the block was transposed), will change the number of cases and variables in the data file:

Note that when you transpose a file, case names become variable names and variable names become case names (for details, press *F1* to access the on-line documentation).

How to automatically fill ranges of data in the spreadsheet:

In addition to the custom-defined operations of filling specific ranges of data with values, available via the data transformation options (see page 81),

spreadsheet-style "fill block" options are available. First, select a block to be filled in the spreadsheet. Then, use the *Fill Block* option accessible from the data spreadsheet *Edit* menu. A hierarchical menu will allow you to select either the *Fill Down* or *Fill Right* option.

The former will copy (duplicate) the first row of the block to all remaining rows; the latter will copy the first column of the block to the remaining columns. Both options work in a manner similar to MS Excel's *Fill Right* and *Fill Down* facility (also available in Excel from the *Edit* menu).

What is the difference between the *Output header* and the *File headers*?

Output header. The output header is an optional one line of text which you can enter into the *Output Header* field of the *Page/Output Setup* dialog (see page 71). The text can be used to identify the current project or stage of data analysis and it will appear in the running head of your reports. It will be in effect as long as you do not change it (even after you turn off the computer).

File headers. The file *One-line Header* (an optional one-line summary title or other identification of the data set) as well as *File Information/Notes* (a paragraph of comments) are stored along with the data file and can be entered or edited in the *Data File Header and Info* dialog, accessible from the *Header...* option in the spreadsheet pull-down menu *Edit* (or by double-clicking on the title field of the spreadsheet displaying the header).

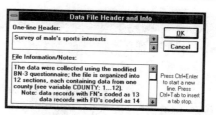

The one-line header is automatically used in reports and graphs produced from the respective data set. For example, it is included in printed reports if the selected report style is set to at least the *Short* setting (see page 71).

The header is also transferred to the title field of custom graphs created from the spreadsheet (see page 38); it can also be automatically included in the title fields of all graphs created using the *Stats Graphs* facilities (in the pull-down menu *Graphs*, see also page 106).

The *File Information/Notes* can be reviewed in the dialog shown above (accessible by double-clicking on the title field of the data spreadsheet) and printed, if requested, in the data printing options dialog (see page 105).

How to set up DDE (*Dynamic Data Exchange*) links between STATISTICA and files created by other Windows applications:

You can establish DDE (*Dynamic Data Exchange*) links between a "source" (or server) file (e.g., a MS Excel spreadsheet or a document written in MS Word) and a STATISTICA data file (the "client" file), so that when changes are made to the data in the source file, the data will be automatically updated in the STATISTICA spreadsheet (client file).

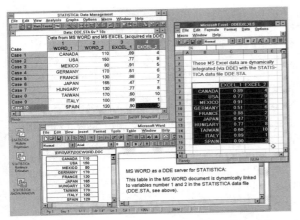

A common application for dynamically linking two files would be in industrial settings, where the STATISTICA data file would be dynamically linked with a measurement device (e.g., in order to automatically update specific measurements hourly). DDE links can be established using the quick, "paste-like" *Paste Link* option in the spreadsheet pull-down menu *Edit*, or by entering a definition of the link into the *Long name (label, formula, link):* field of the *Variable Specifications* dialog.

Refer to the on-line documentation (accessible by pressing *F1* from either of the two options) for details and examples. When a link is established, it can be managed using the *Links Manager* (accessible via the *Links...* option in the spreadsheet pull-down menu *Edit*).

There are also other applications for the DDE data integration facilities in STATISTICA; see the on-line documentation on DDE for details.

How much disk space is necessary to perform data base management operations?

In order to allow the user to revert back to the original data file after file editing, STATISTICA creates temporary and backup files. Thus, in order to edit a data file, the program will need at least twice as much free disk space as the size of the file to be edited. Some operations (e.g., import/export) use intermediate scratch files, thus they may need additional space.

How are the *Case Selection Conditions* stored/saved?

Currently-specified *Case Selection Conditions* (definitions of subsets of data) are automatically stored by STATISTICA when you change modules. You can also save and open them (and maintain libraries of *Case Selection Conditions*) by using the *Open* or *Save As* buttons in the *Case Selection Conditions* dialog (see page 73).

Note that the text of saved *Case Selection Conditions* can also be used in all STATISTICA facilities which allow you to define subsets of cases. For example, the same conventions apply to the data *Recoding* facility (available by pressing the spreadsheet button number 3, see page 34, see also page 83), data verification facilities (available in the *Data Management* module, see page 80), or all procedures which allow you to custom-define multiple subsets of data (such as frequency tables, or multiple-subset scatterplots).

How to review and edit variable specifications (names, formats, notes, formulas, etc.):

Specifications of a single variable. Double-clicking on the variable name in the spreadsheet will open a variable specifications dialog where you can change the variable name, format, missing data value, long label, formula (see page 81), or a DDE link (see page 87) for the current variable. (As in most other facilities commonly used in STATISTICA, alternatively, this dialog can also be accessed from the toolbar, flying menus called by the right-mouse-button, and the pull-down menus.)

The dialog can also be used to access graphs, descriptive statistics, and a listing of sorted numeric and text values for the current variable (press the button *Graphs*). From this dialog, you can also access the *Text Value Manager* (press the *Text Values* button) to review and change the assignments between the text and numeric values for the current variable (see the next three topics).

Specifications of all variables. You can also press the *Variable Specifications* button (button number 2 on the spreadsheet toolbar, see page 34 or the *All Specs* button in the dialog shown above), to bring up an editable, combined table of specifications of all variables in the current data file.

The table format is convenient when you need to compare or edit specifications of several variables, especially when you need to paste and copy between variables (e.g., comments, formulas, or links).

What is the "double notation" (text/numeric) of values?

In STATISTICA, each value may have two identities: numeric (e.g., *1*) and text (e.g., *Male*). This double notation simplifies the use of text values. For example, when entering data, you could enter the values *1* and *2* in variable *Gender* to refer to males and females, respectively. Later, you can type *Male* into any cell containing a *1*, and at the point when you complete the entry, all *1*'s in this column will automatically change to *Male*. In other words, because *1* did not have a text equivalent, the program will understand that you intended to assign the text value *Male* to *1* in this variable. You can repeat the same steps for *2* and *Female*. This feature simplifies entering text values; at the same time you do not lose any advantages of using the numeric data (they can still be used in subsequent numeric analyses). For more information, see also the next paragraph.

How to enter/edit the assignments between numeric and text values:

Normally, the assignments between text and numeric values are handled automatically as you enter or edit data in the spreadsheet (see the previous paragraph). However, in some circumstances, you may want to review, edit or restructure all assignments of values for a particular variable or copy text/numeric assignments from one variable to another. These

StatSoft™

operations can be performed in the *Text Value Manager* (accessible by pressing its respective button on the spreadsheet toolbar, see button number 15, page 37), by pressing the *Text Values* button in the variable specifications dialog for a particular variable (see page 89); or from a flying menu (accessible by pressing the right-mouse-button anywhere on the respective variable in the spreadsheet).

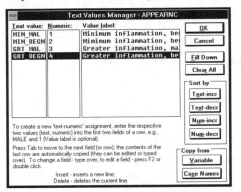

The *Text Value Manager* allows you to sort the assignments by text or numeric values, perform the *Fill Down* operation (to automatically reassign numeric values to text values), *Copy* numeric/text assignments from other variables or from case names, and perform other operations (press *F1* in this dialog to access the on-line documentation).

How to switch between displaying text and numeric values in the data spreadsheet:

As explained in the previous two topics, STATISTICA supports a double notation of values, where each value of a particular variable can simultaneously have a numeric and text identity. You can select a display of text or numeric values using a toggle switch button ![ABC button] on the spreadsheet toolbar (see button number 5, page 35).

How to copy a set of numeric/text value assignments and long value labels to other variables and other files:

One of the options available in the *Text Value Manager* allows you to copy to the current variable the text values from other variables or from case names (see the *Copy from* box in the *Text Value Manager* dialog, above). When you need to copy the numeric/text value assignments and long value labels from one file to another, use the *Merge files* facility (in the *Data Management* module). One of the merge options available from the merge type selection dialog allows you to concatenate or replace text values with values from another file (see the topic on this merge option, page 80).

What is the quickest way to review basic descriptive statistics for a variable in the spreadsheet or Scrollsheet?

Highlight any cell in the desired variable in the spreadsheet (or Scrollsheet), then press the toolbar

button *Quick Stats Graphs* ![Quick Stats Graphs button] (see page 40) to bring up the menu of statistical graphs and options. Alternatively, press the right-mouse-button and select *Quick Stats Graphs* from the flying menu.

Then, double-click on the *Values/Stats of...* option (or highlight this option and press *Enter*). The resulting window will display information about the selected

StatSoft™

variable, a sorted list of its values, and descriptive statistics.

The descriptive statistics can be copied to the Clipboard by pressing the *Copy* button (see the lower part of the window).

What is the quickest way to review ordinal descriptive statistics (median, quartiles) for a variable in the spreadsheet or Scrollsheet?

Highlight any cell in the desired variable in the spreadsheet (or Scrollsheet), then press the toolbar

button *Quick Stats Graphs*  (see page 40). Alternatively, press the right-mouse-button and select *Quick Stats Graphs* from the flying menu which will pop up. Either method will bring up the menu of statistical graphs and options.

Depending on what kind of descriptive statistics you would like to review, select one of the *Box-Whisker of...* options for a single variable (e.g., to review ordinal descriptive statistics and the range, select the option *Median/Quart/Range*):

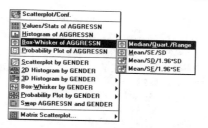

The graph will appear on the screen, including the specific values of the respective descriptive statistics.

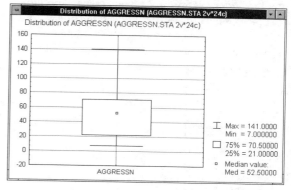

For a more complete description of the distribution of the variable, you can paste into the graph the basic descriptive statistics (copied from the dialog shown in the previous topic):

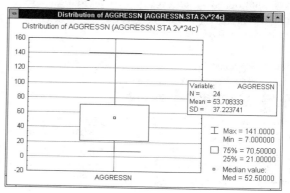

Note that many other statistical graphs of distributions of variables (e.g., a large selection of user-defined, univariate and multivariate box and whiskers plots with outliers) can be requested from

StatSoft™

the *Stats Graphs* menu (available in the pull-down menu *Graphs*).

What is the quickest way to review a sorted list of all values of a variable?

Make sure that the cursor is (anywhere) on the desired variable in the spreadsheet (or Scrollsheet). Press the *Quick Stats Graphs* button on the toolbar. From the *Quick Stats Graphs* menu (see the previous two topics), select the option *Values/Stats of...* . A sorted list of all numeric- and corresponding text-values (if there are any) for that variable will appear.

Note that the assignments between the numeric and text values for the variable can be edited in the *Text Value Manager* (see page 89).

How to change the *Missing Data* code for individual variables:

The value used to designate missing data values for individual variables can be changed in all variable specification dialogs (the default value is *-9999*, see page 78; see also the section on reviewing and editing variable specifications, page 89).

How to rearrange blocks of data or ranges of cases and variables in a data file:

There are two types of those operations: Clipboard-based and *Global*; they operate differently and may produce different effects.

Clipboard-based operations. Clipboard-based operations (invoked via the standard Clipboard keyboard, toolbar, or menu-commands) affect only the *contents* of blocks of data, rows, or columns, and they do not influence the overall size of the data file (e.g., they may empty a column but will not remove the column from the spreadsheet).

The *Global* operations. The *Global* operations option (accessible from the pull-down menu or the spreadsheet toolbar buttons *Vars* and *Cases*, see page 34) are performed on entire rows or columns as "units;" for example, they will move or delete entire columns and not only their contents. Refer to page 34 for more information on those differences.

Note that both types of operations can be initiated by options from the spreadsheet flying menus (use the right-mouse-button).

How to access data from Excel and other foreign data files:

Clipboard. The quickest, and in many cases easiest way to access data files from other Windows applications (e.g., spreadsheets) is to use the Clipboard, which in STATISTICA supports special Clipboard data formats generated by applications such as MS Excel or Lotus for Windows. For example, STATISTICA will properly interpret formatted cells (such as *1,000,000* or *$10*) and text values.

File import facilities. Data files from a wide variety of Windows and non-Windows applications can also be accessed and translated into the STATISTICA format using the file import facilities

(in the *Data Management* module) which also include options to access formatted and free format text (ASCII) files.

The main advantages of using the file import facilities (over the Clipboard) are that:

- They allow the user to specify the exact way in which the translation is to be performed (e.g., access named ranges in the foreign data files, decide whether or not to import variable names, text values, and case names, and how to interpret them); and

- They allow the user to access types of data which are not (or not easily) accessible to Clipboard operations (such as long value labels, special missing data codes) or multiple components of such compound data files as 3D worksheets of Lotus 1-2-3 for Windows.

DDE links. Finally, STATISTICA supports the *Dynamic Data Exchange* conventions, thus you can dynamically link a range of data in its spreadsheet to a subset of data in other (true Windows) applications. The procedure is in fact much simpler than it might appear, and may be easily employed without technical knowledge about the mechanics of DDE, especially when you use the *Paste Link* (instead of the script-entry) method. See the section on DDE (page 87) for an overview, and the on-line documentation for details.

Formats of *Date* values. In STATISTICA data files (which follow a "data-base style" organization), value display formats apply to entire variables and not individual cells (like in Excel). Therefore, values which were formatted as dates in Excel will be displayed in STATISTICA as Julian (integer) values (e.g., *34092* instead of *May 3, 1993*) unless you set the format of the appropriate variables to *Date* (see page 84).

How to export data from STATISTICA to Excel and other foreign data files:

The Clipboard and data file translation facilities described in the previous topic in the context of importing foreign file formats can also be used to export data from STATISTICA to other formats. The same selection of formats and data types is supported when importing data to and exporting them from STATISTICA (see the previous topic).

Can I open more than one input data file simultaneously?

Different data files can be used simultaneously for input in different modules (as mentioned before, different modules can process the same or different data files). In one module, only one file at a time can be used as the main input data file and reside in the data spreadsheet; other files can be opened simultaneously for reference only, thus, they can be opened only as Scrollsheets (if they were previously saved into Scrollsheet files).

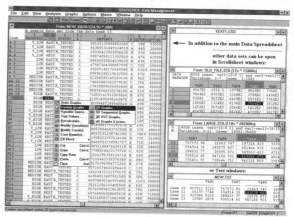

Refer to the section on differences between spreadsheets and Scrollsheets for more information (see page 97).

StatSoft™

Multiple *Megafile Manager* files can be opened simultaneously in the *Data Management* module, allowing you to easily move data from standard STATISTICA data files to different aggregated (or archival) data bases, or to create STATISTICA data files from data stored in various *Megafile Manger* data bases (see page 95).

Can matrix data (e.g., correlations or covariances) instead of raw data be used for input?

Yes, STATISTICA supports a variety of matrix-file types as input data (e.g., for *Regression*, *Factor Analysis*, *Reliability*, and other modules). Matrices of up to 300x300 can be processed. Matrix files can be edited in the spreadsheet (as if they were raw data files), however, in order to be properly interpreted as matrices by the program, they need to meet specific content and format conditions (depending on the matrix type). Refer to the respective module of STATISTICA for details on matrix file input (press *F1* or use the *Help* menu for specific descriptions of the matrix file formats supported by STATISTICA).

In what circumstances does STATISTICA issue the *"Disk full"* message?

STATISTICA uses the disk drive which is designated for temporary files in your Windows configuration for its temporary files. On some systems, this disk may be a RAM drive of a relatively small size. The limited space on that drive may be quickly used up (by STATISTICA and other Windows applications) and the *Disk full* message issued even though there is still free space on some other drive. To check the current setting, look for the *SET TEMP=* line in your *autoexec.bat* file (in the root directory of the boot disk). To remedy the situation, set the location for temporary files to your largest disk. (Note also that because the MS Windows system and various Windows applications use large temporary disk files,

the actual amount of disk space effectively available to an application may be much smaller than the amount reported by *File Manager* immediately after starting the computer.)

What are the differences between the data management options accessible in every module and the *Data Management* module?

Most of the commonly-used data management facilities are integrated with the spreadsheet and available from the data spreadsheet in every module (either from the toolbar, pull-down menu *Edit*, or the flying menus). These commonly-available facilities include all spreadsheet operations on cases and variables, transposing data, data transformations through the spreadsheet formulas and the on-line recoding facilities, ranking, filling ranges, shifting, DDE (*Dynamic Data Exchange*), management of text values, date values, long value labels, and many other options.

The *Data Management* module includes all of these options and, in addition, some more specialized data management facilities, such as the Quick MML programming language (see page 82), interactive data verification and cleaning facility (see page 80), and others.

Access to *Megafile Manager* facilities. In addition, the *Data Management* module of STATISTICA provides access to all facilities of the *Megafile Manager* data base system (see the next topic), which offers options to access and process data in unusual data formats (e.g., data organized into extremely large records or data with very long text values). A unique feature of *Megafile Manager* is that it can process data with extremely long records (up to 8 megabytes per record). *Megafile Manager* also can be used as an archival data base system to store data combined from various sources (preserving their original formats). Easy to use (one step) and

flexible facilities are provided in the *Data Management* module to move data in and out, between STATISTICA data files and archival *Megafile Manager* data bases.

What is Megafile Manager?

Overview. *Megafile Manager* is a specialized data base management system accessible from the *Data Management* module of STATISTICA (see the previous topic). Its unique feature is that it can manage and directly process types of data which need to be transformed, aggregated, extracted, or cleaned before they can be directly accessed by any statistical or graphics procedures of STATISTICA (e.g., data embedded inside very long text values or data organized into very long records).

case). Data organized in such long records can be produced by some automated quality control measurement devices or other data acquisition or monitoring equipment. Also, such files are sometimes useful in maintaining integrated, large archival data banks consisting of numerous merged or concatenated files.

Maintaining large, archival data banks; hierarchical relations between data bases. *Megafile Manager* offers numerous options for aggregating data sets from other applications and setting up efficient archival data bases. It also supports links between related (and hierarchically organized) data sets. Subsets of variables from such archival data banks can be extracted and used with other applications (such as STATISTICA, Excel, or Paradox).

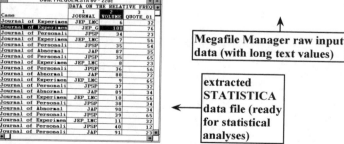

Megafile Manager raw input data (with long text values)

extracted STATISTICA data file (ready for statistical analyses)

Megafile Manager can process extremely large records of data (*cases*): up to 32,000 variables with up to 255 characters each (up to 8 megabytes per

Preprocessing large records of raw data. Another unique application of *Megafile Manager* is at the stage of analysis when raw data need to be aggregated or preprocessed before meaningful indices are obtained for use in data analysis. Such raw data sets (e.g., from automated quality control measurement devices or other data acquisition equipment) may feature records that are too long to fit into any standard application (e.g., 32,000 measures per case). *Megafile Manager* can be used to access such data sets, convert them into meaningful indices, and transfer to another application (such as STATISTICA) for further analysis. Such raw data often need to be cleaned and verified before they can be preprocessed.

Data processing, analysis, *MML* language. Thus, *Megafile Manager* not only offers facilities to

aggregate, store, and maintain long-record files, but it can also efficiently process them. Its integrated programming language (*MML*) features a variety of data analytic options, custom-defined recoding functions and a large library of functions which can be expanded by adding new, user-defined procedures. *Megafile Manager* also includes integrated basic statistics facilities that can process data regardless of the record size. For example, it can tabulate or compute descriptive statistics, and generate correlation matrices of practically unlimited size (the size of correlation matrices that could be generated by *Megafile Manager* exceeds the capacity of any existing storage device).

Long text values. As mentioned before, another specific feature of *Megafile Manager* is its facilities to process very long text values (see the illustration above). Also, its integrated programming language (*MML*) offers a comprehensive selection of functions to manipulate text data.

Exchanging data with STATISTICA data files. *Megafile Manager* uses a specialized file format optimized for its specific applications (and capable of storing data from other applications in their original formats). However, easy to use (one step) and flexible facilities are provided in the *Data Management* module to move data in and out, between STATISTICA data files and archival *Megafile Manager* data bases.

Scrollsheets (Scrollable Tables with Results)

What are Scrollsheets?

In STATISTICA, all numeric and text output is displayed in spreadsheet-like windows called Scrollsheets. Their content can be anything from a short line to megabytes of output, and they offer a variety of options to facilitate reviewing the results and visualizing them in predefined and custom-defined graphs (for an overview and illustrations, see page 13 of this manual).

What is the difference between Scrollsheets and spreadsheets?

All differences between these two--on the surface very similar--main types of "documents" in STATISTICA are related to the difference in their contents: Scrollsheets are used to display results from analyses, whereas spreadsheets hold input data files. Both types of tables look similar and they offer very similar facilities, including the graphics options (both *Custom* and *Stats* graphs, see page 106, are available from Scrollsheets and from spreadsheets). However, each of them offers specialized facilities which are applicable to their respective contents. For example, data spreadsheets feature integrated data management, restructuring, transformation and recoding facilities (see page 34), whereas Scrollsheets offer specialized graphs related to the types of statistical output they contain or integrated facilities to identify cells or rows containing results which meet particular statistical criteria (e.g., significance level).

Toolbars, flying menus. These differences and similarities are reflected in the appearance of the toolbars which accompany each of the two types of document-windows (see page 33 and page 44), as well as in the contents of the flying menus which can be brought up by clicking the right-mouse-button on individual cells. Note that these two types of documents can easily be converted into one another (see the next two paragraphs).

Converting data spreadsheets into Scrollsheets. The *Make Scrollsheet...* option (see the spreadsheet *File* menu; keyboard shortcut is *F11*) can be used to convert the data file or the currently highlighted block of data into a Scrollsheet; an intermediate dialog will allow you to select options. A data file saved this way into a Scrollsheet can later be opened (e.g., for reference) at any point of the data analysis without affecting the main data file residing in the data spreadsheet and used as input data (the default file name extension for Scrollsheet files is **.scr*).

Converting Scrollsheets into standard data files (spreadsheets). The *Save as Data...* option (see the Scrollsheet *File* menu) can be used to convert the contents of the current Scrollsheet or the currently highlighted block into a standard STATISTICA data file. A data file created this way can later be opened for input as a regular data file, thus allowing you to submit output from one analysis as input for another.

What is the Scrollsheet queue?

Queues of Scrollsheets (and graphs). Statistical analyses may produce large amounts of output. Scrollsheets offer flexible ways to organize the output regardless of its size. New Scrollsheets are generated by subsequent analyses in a "queue," where older Scrollsheets are closed automatically as new ones are created (to avoid having too many open windows at once). The Scrollsheets are closed on a first-in-first-out basis, and the default length of the queue is 3. In other words, when the fourth Scrollsheet is created, then the first one is closed (with no warning unless you have edited or customized it). The same queue conventions apply to graph windows.

Note that an option is provided to automatically print (or send to the output file and/or the on-screen *Text/output Window*) each Scrollsheet which is generated on the screen (see below).

Auto-report (*Automatically Print All Scrollsheets*).

In order to create a log of all Scrollsheets, select the *Automatically Print All Scrollsheets (Auto-report)* option in the *Page/Output Setup* dialog (accessible in the pull-down menu *File* or by double-clicking on the *Output* field on the status bar at the bottom of the STATISTICA window; see page 71).

In the same dialog, you will be able to specify where to direct the output: to the printer, a disk text output file, or the scrollable *Text/output Window*, and adjust other output settings.

The length of the queues.

In some instances, you may want to increase the length of this queue. Use the *Scrollsheet Manager* in the pull-down menu *Window* to temporarily change the length of the queue for the current session (the setting will return to the default length when you close the current module of STATISTICA):

In addition, the *Scrollsheet Manager* dialog (see above) can be used to "lock" specific Scrollsheets (see the next two topics).

The pull-down menu *Options* can be used to adjust the queue length permanently (the default length of the Scrollsheet queue is 3 windows):

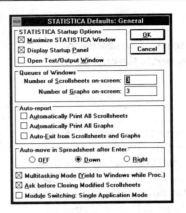

How to keep a Scrollsheet from being replaced in the queue:

Regardless of the length of the queue, you can "lock" individual windows (i.e., "remove" them from the queue; use the *Scrollsheet Manger* accessible from the pull-down menu *Window*, shown in the previous topic), so that they will not be automatically closed as long as you do not exit the program.

What is the difference between *locking* and *saving* Scrollsheets?

Locking a Scrollsheet (see above) will preserve the Scrollsheet as long as you do not close the current module. Saving Scrollsheets (see below) allows you to preserve them across analyses (e.g., in different modules or sessions), because saved Scrollsheets can be opened again at any point of the analysis in any STATISTICA module. Also, saved Scrollsheets (file name extension *.scr) can be printed in batch using the *Print Files...* facility (in the pull-down menu *File*, see page 101).

How to save a Scrollsheet:

Saving Scrollsheets in a Scrollsheet format.

Use option *Save* (*Shift+F12*) or *Save As...* (*F12*) in the *File* menu. By default, Scrollsheets are saved in the Scrollsheet file format (file name extension **.scr*); saved Scrollsheets can be opened again at any point of the analysis in any STATISTICA module. Such Scrollsheet files also can be printed in batch using the *Print Files...* facility (in the pull-down menu *File*, see page 101).

Saving Scrollsheets as data files.

Use the option *Save as Data...* in the *File* menu to save a Scrollsheet as a standard STATISTICA data file which can then be used for input in subsequent analyses (file name extension **.sta*).

For information on the differences between spreadsheets and Scrollsheets, refer to the respective section on page 97.

How to add rows or columns to the current Scrollsheet:

Use the options *Append Columns...* and *Append Rows...* in the Scrollsheet pull-down menu *Edit*. The extra space can be used for notes or input pasted from the Clipboard.

How to select (highlight) the entire Scrollsheet:

Following the standard spreadsheet convention, click in the upper left corner of the Scrollsheet. This shortcut is useful, for example, when you intend to copy the entire file to the Clipboard.

Note that by clicking twice in the same area, you will de-select (i.e., select and then de-select) the entire Scrollsheet.

How to de-select a block in the Scrollsheet:

Click twice in the upper left corner of the Scrollsheet. The first click will select the entire Scrollsheet, the second one will de-select it including the block that was marked.

Alternatively, you could press *Ctrl+1* or double-click anywhere on the Scrollsheet (as if you intended to edit a cell); this will also de-select the block.

How to edit the contents of a Scrollsheet cell (and not overwrite it):

Double-click on the cell. To avoid clearing the contents of the cell (at the point when you start entering a correction), first double-click on the cell before you start typing. This will enter the *editing mode* and will position the cursor within the cell.

Press *F2*. Alternatively, you can follow the standard spreadsheet convention and press *F2*, which will also enter the edit mode for the currently highlighted cell.

What graphs are available from Scrollsheets?

There are two general types of graphs available directly from all Scrollsheets: *Custom* graphs (which allow you to custom-design graphs from the contents of the Scrollsheets to produce user-defined visualizations of results) and *Quick Stats Graphs* (which are predefined, general-purpose statistical graphs and specialized graphs related to the output presented in the current Scrollsheet). Refer to page 46 for descriptions of graphs available from the spreadsheet toolbar, and to page 106 for more information on differences between *Quick Stats Graphs*, *Stats Graphs* and *Custom Graphs*.

How to make a Scrollsheet from a data file:

When you are in the data spreadsheet, press *F11* (or select the *Make Scrollsheet...* option from the pull-down menu *File*). The subsequent dialog will allow you to select a subset (by default, all data will be included, unless a block is currently selected). A Scrollsheet containing the selected data will be created. You can save it in a Scrollsheet file (file name extension **.scr*) which can be opened at any point without affecting the main data file selected for input in the current analysis. For information on differences between spreadsheets and Scrollsheets, see the respective section on page 97.

Saving and Printing Reports

How to print text reports from analyses:

The simplest way to print a Scrollsheet is to press the *Print* button on the toolbar. If an output channel is not selected, then STATISTICA will open the *Page/Output Setup* dialog (see page 71) and ask you where to send the output (to the printer, disk file, and/or the *Text/output Window*). No other intermediate option dialogs will be displayed. The entire Scrollsheet will be sent to the output. If a block is selected in the Scrollsheet, then only that block will be sent to the output destination.

More options are available when you use the *Print...* (or *F4*) option in the pull-down menu *File*. The *Print Scrollsheet* options dialog will appear allowing you to customize various aspects of the Scrollsheet printing, such as how to treat marked cells, etc.

Automatic reports. Note that if you intend to keep a complete log of all Scrollsheets which are displayed on the screen without having to remember to print them, select the *Automatically Print All Scrollsheets (Auto-report)* option in the *Page/Output Setup* dialog, accessible by double-clicking on the *Output* field on the status bar at the bottom of the STATISTICA window (see page 71).

Other options. In the same *Page/Output Setup* dialog, you will be able to specify where to direct the output (printer, disk-output file, and/or the scrollable *Text/output Window*). Refer to the section on the status bar *Output* field (page 71) for information about report styles, formatting options, printing gridlines, and other output options.

How to print multiple Scrollsheets previously saved in the Scrollsheet files:

In order to print a set of previously-saved Scrollsheets (and/or graphs) in batch , use the *Print Files* option available from the pull-down menu *File*.

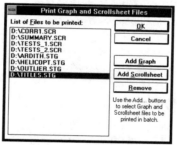

Use the *Add Scrollsheet* and/or the *Add Graph* buttons in the *Print Graph and Scrollsheet Files* dialog (see above) to select the desired Scrollsheets (and/or graphs), and click *OK* to begin the batch printing process. All of the selected graphs will be printed first (on separate pages, in the order in which they are selected), and then all of the Scrollsheets will be printed together (in the order in which they are selected).

For more information on selecting Scrollsheets and/or graphs for the batch printing, see the on-line *electronic manual* (click *F1* in this dialog).

How to adjust margins in the text reports:

Use the *Text Output Margins* dialog (accessible by pressing the *Margins* button in the *Page/Output Setup* dialog (accessible by double-clicking on the *Output*

field on the status bar at the bottom of the STATISTICA window, see page 71).

You can position the desired text (e.g., from spreadsheets, Scrollsheets, or the *Text/output Window*) on the printed page by adjusting the margins (specify the *Left*, *Top*, *Right*, and *Bottom* margin widths) according to a specific measure (*Percent*, *Centimeter*, or *Inch*).

Note that these margin settings are independent from the margin settings for the graphics output (which can be adjusted in the *Print Preview* or *Graph Margins* dialogs).

How to suppress the printing of gridlines in tables:

The list box *Lines* in the *Page/Output Setup* dialog (accessible by double-clicking on the *Output* field on the status bar at the bottom of the STATISTICA window, see page 71) allows you to control the thickness of lines printed in tables. Selecting the top setting in the list (the empty field) will suppress the lines (see also the next topic).

How to change the character-lines into continuous lines in report tables:

Tables printed in STATISTICA. If gridlines of any width are requested in reports, the lines are always printed in STATISTICA as continuous high-resolution lines and not character lines (see the *Page/Output Setup* dialog, accessible by double-clicking on the *Output* field on the status bar at the bottom of the STATISTICA window, page 71). The character lines will be produced only in the

Text/output Window or text file output, where high-resolution lines are not drawn (to allow that output to be edited with all word processors and text editors).

STATISTICA tables printed in word processors. If instead of printing the reports in STATISTICA (featuring high-resolution gridlines in tables), you need to include high-resolution tables in your word processor documents, it is recommended to use the Clipboard to copy the desired Scrollsheets and spreadsheets and paste them into word processor documents. If pasted this way, STATISTICA Scrollsheets and spreadsheets will appear as tab-delimited tables, compatible with table generators in Windows word processors (e.g., MS Word).

The vertical gridlines do not show properly in printed tables; how do I change the printer setup?

Enable the *Print TrueType as Graphics* option in the *Setup/Options* dialog of *Printer Setup...* (pull-down menu *File*). The setup programs for some drivers contain this switch in the *Options...* dialog.

How to add custom headers to printed output:

One line of text can be added to the fixed report header (including the name of the module, page number, and the optional time and date). Enter the text to be used as the header into the *Output Header* field in the *Page/Output Setup* dialog (accessible by double-clicking on the *Output* field on the status bar at the bottom of the STATISTICA window, see page 71).

The text will be printed in the second line from the top of every page of the report. This text will also be automatically saved by STATISTICA even when you turn off the computer and it will be included in reports as long as you do not change it.

How to automatically print (or save to report files) all Scrollsheets from an analysis:

The *Auto-report* option. Enable the *Automatically Print All Scrollsheets (Auto-report)* switch in the *Page/Output Setup* dialog (accessible by double-clicking on the *Output* field on the status bar at the bottom of the STATISTICA window, see page 71). This mode will automatically generate a text-log of all Scrollsheets displayed on the screen, releasing you from having to press the *Printer* button in order to print individual Scrollsheets.

The contents of every Scrollsheet generated on the screen are automatically sent to the current output channel (the printer, disk file, and/or the *Text/output Window*) following the report style and conventions defined in that dialog.

"Automatic pressing" of the *Continue* button to speed up batch output. When, instead of reviewing the output on-screen, you need to quickly produce a hard copy (or a disk-output file), then it is advantageous to select the *Auto-Exit from Scrollsheets and Graphs* option in the *Defaults: General* dialog (option *General...* in the pull-down menu *Options*). If that option is selected, STATISTICA will "internally" press the *Continue* button on every graph and Scrollsheet, thus allowing you to print long sequences of Scrollsheets without having to press the *Continue* button at the end of every "queue-full" of Scrollsheets.

For example, if an analysis produces 10 Scrollsheets and the current Scrollsheet queue is set to 3 (default), then STATISTICA will stop after displaying every 3 Scrollsheets and wait for you to press the *Continue* button, regardless of whether the Scrollsheets are automatically sent to the output or not. However, when the *Auto-Exit from Scrollsheets and Graphs* option is selected, then all 10 Scrollsheets will be displayed (and printed) one after another without prompting you for any input.

How to speed up printing reports:

Turn off option *Automatically Eject Each Page*. This option is included in the *Page/Output Setup* dialog (accessible by double-clicking on the *Output* field on the status bar at the bottom of the STATISTICA window, see page 71). When the *Automatically Eject Each Page* option is enabled (a default setting), then each page of the printout is finalized as soon as it is full. Thus, this mode is somewhat slower overall, as the process of printing is initiated for each page separately; however, its advantage is that it automatically produces hard copies as your analysis progresses (which may be desired in some circumstances). Alternatively, when this switch is turned off, all output is accumulated in an internal buffer and printed more economically all at once at the end of the session (or whenever you select the *Print/Eject Current Pages* option in the pull-down menu *File*, which allows you to "flush out" the current contents of the output buffer at any point).

Do not use the high-resolution printer settings for table gridlines. Note that table gridlines are printed as high-resolution graphics, thus the output is faster when the gridlines are suppressed (set the *Lines* field to the empty field setting, see page 102). If you wish to print gridlines, it is recommended to set the requested printer resolution in the *Printer Setup...* dialog for STATISTICA's text output (see pull-down menu *File*) to no more than 150 DPI (on non-Postscript printers). This will speed up printing and at the same time will not affect the quality of the output, because the fonts will still print at the highest resolution. Note also that in STATISTICA, the printer settings for text output can be adjusted independently of the printer settings for graphs (where the printer resolution will affect the smoothness of curves and thus, you might prefer to maintain a higher-resolution default).

Adjust the report style. If the report style is set to *Medium* or *Long* (in the *Page/Output Setup* dialog, accessible by double-clicking on the *Output* field on

the status bar at the bottom of the STATISTICA window, see page 71), then large amounts of supplementary information about the selected variables are automatically directed to the printer (press *F1* in that dialog to review descriptions of the report styles). The amount of this supplementary information is particularly large when the variables have many text values and long text value labels. Changing to a more economical style (e.g., *Short*) will speed up printing.

How is the *disk file output* different from the printed output?

If the output is set to *FILE* (in the *Page/Output Setup* dialog, accessible by double-clicking on the *Output* field on the status bar at the bottom of the STATISTICA window, see page 71) then STATISTICA will ask you for the name of an output file, and then direct to that file a text representation of all output. The contents of the reports directed to the output file are identical to those which are printed (if the output is set to *PRINTER*), with one difference mentioned below.

Gridlines in tables. The only difference between the printer and file output is that unlike in the printed output, character (instead of continuous) table gridlines are produced in disk file reports to assure their compatibility with all word processors and text editors. (Refer to page 102 for information on how to print STATISTICA tables with high-resolution gridlines in word processors.)

Continuous reports from different modules.
The output continues to the same output file as you switch modules of STATISTICA. Moreover, if you do not turn off the output before exiting the program, next time when you start STATISTICA, it will automatically open the last used output file and continue appending the new output to it.

Changing output files. You can close the output file and start a new one at any point via the

Page/Output Setup dialog (accessible by double-clicking on the *Output* field in the status bar on the bottom of the STATISTICA window, see page 71). Press the *Output file* button and enter the new output file name.

When the output file cannot be edited. Note that an output file cannot be edited (e.g., cannot be opened in the STATISTICA text editor) at the same time that it is open for output. You can edit it only after it is closed. If you wish to edit that file, close it first by turning off the file output or selecting a new file for output (see the previous paragraph).

What is the difference between the output to the on-screen *Text/output Window* and a *disk-output file*?

These two output channels can be open simultaneously, and they receive the same output (selectable in the *Page/Output Setup* dialog, accessible by double-clicking on the *Output* field on the status bar at the bottom of the STATISTICA window, see page 71). However, they differ in several ways.

Disk-output files. The disk file output produces permanent report files; the capacity of such reports is limited only by disk space. The reports can be edited using STATISTICA or any other text editor or word processor but not when the file is open by STATISTICA for output (see the previous topic).

On-screen *Text/output Window*. On the other hand, the on-screen *Text/output Window* is like a text editor which is open simultaneously for input from several sources: it receives text from STATISTICA's "printed" output, and at the same time you can add to it your own notes, or edit and supplement it by pasting from the Clipboard. The *Text/output Window* is used as an editable, temporary means to review recent output.

How to print data files:

The simplest way to print a data spreadsheet is to press the *Print* button on the toolbar when the spreadsheet window is active (see page 41). If an output channel is not selected, then STATISTICA will open the *Page/Output Setup* dialog (see page 71) and ask you where to send the output (the printer, disk file, the *Text/output Window*). No other intermediate option dialogs will be displayed. The entire spreadsheet is sent to the output. If a block is selected in the spreadsheet, then only that block will be sent to the output.

More data printing options are available when you use the *Print...* (or *F4*) option in the pull-down menu *File*. The *Print Data* options dialog will appear allowing you to customize the data listing report.

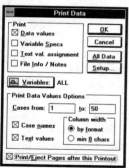

You can specify the subset to be printed (by default, the current block, if one is selected), the types of data and the categories of information about variables to be included, the text of the *Notes* attached to the file, and formatting. Other aspects of the report can be customized in the *Page/Output Setup* dialog (accessible by double-clicking on the *Output* field on the status bar at the bottom of the STATISTICA window, see page 71).

StatSoft™

Graphics

What categories of graphs are available in STATISTICA? What is the difference between *Custom* graphs and *Stats* graphs?

In addition to the specialized graphs which are available from the output dialogs of all statistical procedures, there are two general categories of graphs accessible from menus and toolbars of all Scrollsheets and spreadsheets:

- *Custom Graphs*, and
- *Stats Graphs* (and *Quick Stats Graphs*).

They differ in terms of the source of data which they visualize; the differences are summarized in the following sections.

 **Custom Graphs.** *Custom Graphs* allow you to visualize any custom-defined combination of values from Scrollsheets and spreadsheets (from rows, columns or both, and/or their subsets). When you select one of the four global types of these graphs (*Custom 2D Graphs, Custom 3D Sequential Graphs, Custom 3D XYZ Graphs*, or *Custom nD Graphs and Icons*, see the sections starting on pages 38 and 46), a respective dialog will open allowing you to specify the parts of the current Scrollsheet or spreadsheet to be plotted. The layout of this dialog depends on the global type of the *Custom* graph which you have selected (e.g., *Custom 2D Graphs*). The initial selection of the data to be plotted (suggested in that dialog) depends on the current block (or cursor) position in the current Scrollsheet or spreadsheet. Each of these *Custom* graph definition dialogs allow you to select the specific types of graph (within the global type). However, as described below, the graph type can also

be adjusted later, after the graph is created (via the *General Layout* or *Plot Layout* dialogs accessible by clicking on the graph background or from the graph pull-down menu *Layouts*).

Stats Graphs. Unlike *Custom Graphs* (which provide general tools to create custom visualizations of numerical Scrollsheet output, or spreadsheet data, see above), *Stats Graphs* are pre-defined statistical graphs. They are available from the pull-down menu *Graphs*:

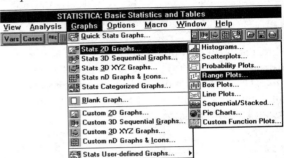

and offer hundreds of types of graphical representations and analytic summaries of data. They are not limited to the values in the current Scrollsheet, and they do not depend on highlighted blocks or the current cursor position; instead, they process data directly from the current data file. They represent either standard methods to graphically summarize raw data (e.g., various scatterplots, histograms, or plots of central tendencies such as medians) or standard graphical analytic techniques (e.g., categorized normal probability plots, detrended probability plots, or plots of confidence intervals of regression lines). As the *Stats Graphs* are generated, STATISTICA will take into account the current case selection and weighting conditions (see pages 73 and 74, respectively) for the variables selected to be plotted.

Quick Stats Graphs. *Quick Stats Graphs* include the most-commonly used types of *Stats Graphs* (which are available from the pull-down

menu *Graphs*, see the previous paragraph). *Quick Stats Graphs* do not offer as many options as *Stats Graphs*, however, they are quicker to select because unlike *Stats Graphs*:

- *Quick Stats Graphs* can be called from flying menus and toolbars (and they do not require any pull-down menu selections),

- *Quick Stats Graphs* do not require the user to select variables (the variable selection is determined by the current cursor position within a Scrollsheet or spreadsheet), and

- *Quick Stats Graphs* do not require the user to select options from any intermediate dialogs (default formats of the respective graphs are produced).

Clicking on the  button on the toolbar, or selecting the *Quick Stats Graphs* option (either from the right-mouse-button flying menu, or the pull-down menu *Graphs*) will open a menu from which you may choose one of the statistical graphs applicable to the current variable, that is, to the variable indicated by the current cursor position in the Scrollsheet or spreadsheet.

In all spreadsheets and those Scrollsheets which involve only one list of variables (and not two lists or one grouping variable and a list), the flying menu will have the following format.

If the Scrollsheet has a matrix format or a format where a cursor position may indicate not one but two variables, then predefined bivariate graphs for the specified pair of variables will be available from the *Quick Stats Graphs* menu (and STATISTICA will not ask you for the selection of the "second" variable for the bivariate graphs).

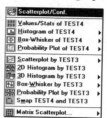

If no variables are indicated by the current cursor position, then selecting any of the *Quick Stats Graphs* will prompt you to select a variable from a list. As the *Quick Stats Graphs* are generated, STATISTICA will take into account the current case selection and weighting conditions (see pages 73 and 74, respectively) for the variables that are being plotted.

Other specialized graphs. In addition to the standard selection of *Quick Stats Graphs* (see above), some Scrollsheets also offer other, more specialized statistical graphs (e.g., icon plots of regression residuals, time sequence plots in *Time Series*, or contour plots in *Cluster Analysis*). As mentioned before, other, specialized statistical graphs which are related not to a specific Scrollsheet but to a type of analysis (e.g., plots of means [e.g., interactions] in *ANOVA/MANOVA*, nonlinear estimation results) are accessible directly from results dialogs (i.e., the dialogs which contain output options from the current analysis).

Are there limits to the customization options available for each of the types of graphs described in the previous topic?

No. Regardless of how a graph was requested or defined, once a graph appears on the screen, all graph customization options available in STATISTICA (see the topic *How to customize graphs*, page 117, below) can be used to customize it. The customization

options available for all graphs also include appending new plots to existing graphs, merging graphs, linking and embedding graphs and artwork, as well as all drawing, fitting, and graph restructuring options. Also, all those options can be used to customize graphs which were saved and later retrieved from disk files.

How to access graphs which visualize raw data:

This topic is a brief summary of the first topic of this section (*What categories of graphs are available in STATISTICA?*).

As mentioned previously, there are several "categories" of graphs available in STATISTICA which visualize raw data (as opposed to visualizations of results of analyses or other graphs based on pre-processed data).

(1) *Custom Graphs*. When requested from the spreadsheet (via toolbars or flying menus, see above), *Custom Graphs* allow you to custom-define any aspects of raw data (cases, variables or both) and represent them in graphs. While selecting these graphs, the user is not confined to any pre-defined formats or layouts.

For example, you can request a scatterplot of data in *Case 1* against data in *Case 145* taking into account only variables number *17* through *225*; or you can request a *3D XYZ plot* of the values of some *cases* against the values of some *variables* (see the first topic in this section for details).

(2) *Quick Stats Graphs*. *Quick Stats Graphs* offer the quickest method to create the most-commonly used (predefined) statistical graphs from spreadsheets or Scrollsheets (e.g., histograms, scatterplots, box and whisker plots, probability plots, etc.).

These graphs are available either from the toolbars or flying menus, and because the selection of variables to be plotted in these graphs is determined by the

current cursor location (within the current spreadsheet or Scrollsheet), *Quick Stats Graphs* require a minimum of input on the part of the user. Most of these graphs require just two clicks of the mouse.

(3) *Stats Graphs*. As opposed to *Quick Stats Graphs* (see the previous paragraph) which are designed to offer the quickest access to the most-commonly used types of statistical graphs (from raw data), *Stats Graphs* (available from the pull-down menu *Graphs*) offer a large variety of graphs and graphical analytic procedures selectable via a user-interface which follows the logic used to specify all statistical or analytic procedures in STATISTICA. This logic is illustrated in the next topic.

How to specify *Stats Graphs*:

As mentioned in the previous topic, STATISTICA's *Stats Graphs* (which are a "superset" of *Quick Stats Graphs*) offer a large variety of graphical analytic procedures selectable via a user-interface which follows the logic used to specify all statistical or analytic procedures in the STATISTICA system.

Example of a complex graph. From the pull-down menu *Graphs*, select the desired *general type* of graph (e.g., *Stats Categorized Graphs...*) and in the respective hierarchical menu select the desired *type* of graph (e.g., *3D Graphs...*):

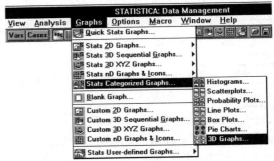

The respective graph definition dialog (in this case, *3D Categorized Plots*) will appear:

StatSoft™

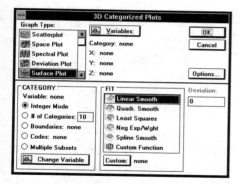

The layout of this dialog is similar to all analysis definition dialogs in STATISTICA (see the introductory example sections at the beginning of this manual). Press the *Variables* button to select the three variables (*X*, *Y*, and *Z*) to be plotted; e.g., *BLOOD_P1*, *BLOOD_P2*, and *CHOLEST*.

Because you requested a categorized graph, you also need to select a categorical (i.e., grouping) variable to be used to divide the data into categories (e.g., *males*, *females*, and *unknown*). In the *CATEGORY* box (see the lower left corner of the dialog), you may also select the method by which the categorical variable will be used to categorize data. By default, all integer values of the categorical variable are used as codes which identify groups (see the setting *Integer Mode*). However, you can also select other methods; for example, you may divide the distribution of the grouping variable into a desired number of intervals (# *of Categories*), define custom intervals (*Boundaries*), or select specific coding values (*Codes*), see page 133 for an overview of categorization methods.

Alternatively, instead of relying on a particular categorical variable, you may select the *Multiple Subsets* categorization method which offers the most flexible way to define categories of data to be plotted. Imagine that you need to include in the first category only *MALE* subjects less than *41* years old, in the second category -- *MALES* older than *40*, and in the third category -- all *FEMALES* regardless of age.

Select the *Multiple Subset* categorization method (see the radio button on the bottom of the *CATEGORY* area); the *Change Variable* button shown above will then change into the *Specify Subsets* button (applicable to the current categorization method). Press that button to bring up the *Specify Multiple Subsets* dialog, and specify the respective conditions as shown below (follow the standard *Case Selection Conditions* conventions as described on page 73):

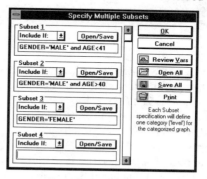

The graph definition dialog will now look as shown below (note that the setting of the *FIT* list box has been changed to the quadratic function (*Quad. Smooth*):

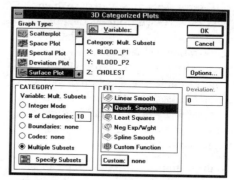

Before you press *OK* to create the graph, you may press the *Options* button (see the upper part of the dialog) and adjust some other settings (e.g., you could request to use text values of some variable in the data set as case labels). For now, however, press *OK* to view the default graph.

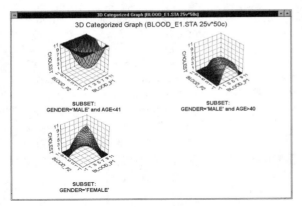

Customization of *Stats Graphs before* vs. *after* a graph is produced. As illustrated in the section *How to customize STATISTICA graphs*, see page 117, below), most graph customization options (hundreds of settings which control virtually all aspects of the appearance of STATISTICA graphs) are interactively accessible *after* a graph is produced, by clicking on specific components of the graph (or from the graph *General Layout* and *Plot Layout* dialogs accessible from the pull-down menu *Layouts*).

However, some of the graph definition or customization features--specifically, those which control how data are accessed from the data file, and what information is extracted from those data (e.g., variables, categorization, value labels, case names, scale value labels)--have to be set before the graph is produced. In this example, the selection of variables, the categorization of cases, and the settings available in the dialog accessible by pressing the *Options* button (not used in this example), had to be set before the graph was produced.

Now, return to the example. Once the graph appears on the screen, you can double-click anywhere on the graph background in order to access the *General Layout* dialog (see page 118) which allows you to customize the global features of the graph:

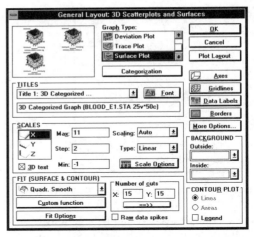

In this dialog, you may change the type of graph to *Contour Plot* (use the *Graph Type* list box), request a legend (check the check box in the lower right corner of the dialog), and increase the *Number of cuts* (i.e., the resolution of the fit used to produce the contour plot) from the default *15x15* to *25x25*:

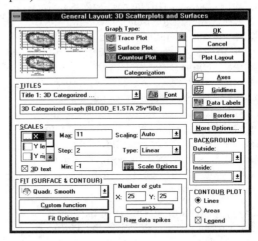

When all settings are adjusted, press *OK* to see the graph:

StatSoft™

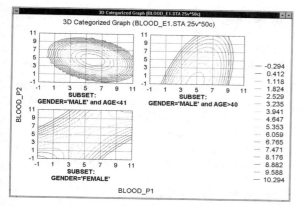

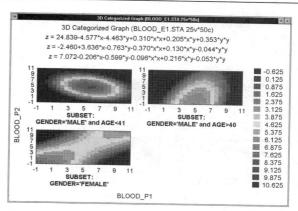

Now, return to the *General Layout* dialog to change the type of contour to *Area*; also, enter the control codes **@F[1,1]**, **@F[1,2]**, and **@F[1,3]** (see page 125), into the first three lines of the graph title in order to display the specific equations describing the quadratic functions fitted to plot number one (see value *1* entered as the first parameter of the control code) in each of the three sub-graphs (see the second parameter entered as *1*, *2*, and *3*, respectively):

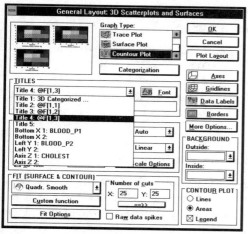

Note that a faster method (offering more formatting options) to display function equations is to request them in the *Options* dialog (accessible from the *Stats Graphs* dialog in which the graph was defined, see page 126). Press *OK* to see the modified graph:

You may now continue to explore other customization facilities in order to further modify the graph. The easiest way to get access to all customization facilities for specific components of graphs is either to double-click on the respective components of the graph (which is the shortcut method to access the most-commonly used customization facility for each component of the graph) or to pull up the flying menu associated with that component by clicking on it with the right-mouse-button.

For example, if you click with the right-mouse-button on any of the graph scales, the following flying menu will offer a selection of options which can be used to customize that particular scale:

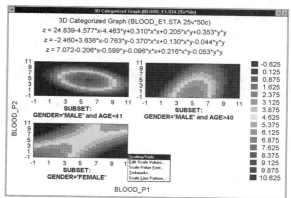

Graph proportions can be adjusted by pressing the graphics window toolbar button number 6 (see page

54); the status of the legend can be changed from the default (*fixed*) to *movable* (see page 121), and the text of the legend can be edited, rearranged and repositioned:

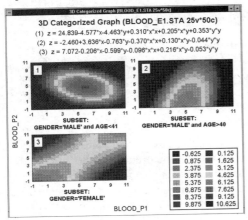

What is the Graph queue?

The queues of graphs. Statistical analyses sometimes produce large numbers of graphs (e.g., cascades of graphs for each combination of variables from two lists). Queues of document windows implemented in STATISTICA offer flexible ways to organize such output regardless of its size. New graphs are generated by subsequent analyses in a "queue," where older graphs are closed automatically as new ones are created (to avoid having too many open windows). The graphs are closed on the first-in-first-out basis, and the default length of the queue is 3. In other words, when the fourth graph is created, then the first one is closed (with no warning unless you have edited or customized it). The same queue conventions apply to Scrollsheet windows. Note that an option is provided to automatically print each graph which is generated on the screen (see below).

Automatically printing all graphs. In order to create a log of all graphs, select the option *Automatically Print All Graphs* in the *Page/Output Setup* dialog (accessible in the pull-down menu *File*

or by double-clicking on the *Output* field on the status bar at the bottom of the STATISTICA window; see page 71). For more information about this option, refer to the section on *Printing Graphs* (page 137).

The length of the queue. In some instances, you may want to increase or decrease the length of this queue. Use the *Graph Manager* in the pull-down menu *Window* to change the length of the queue for the current session (the pull-down menu *Options* can be used to adjust the queue length permanently).

How to keep a graph from being replaced in the queue:

Regardless of the length of the queue, you can also "lock" individual windows (i.e., "remove" them from the queue; use the *Graph Manger* in the pull-down menu *Window*), so that they will not be automatically closed as long as you do not exit the program.

What is the difference between *locking* and *saving* graphs?

Locking a graph (see above) will preserve the graph as long as you do not close the current module. Saving the graph (see below) allows you to preserve it across analyses (e.g., in different modules) or open it again in a future session.

How to save STATISTICA graphs:

STATISTICA graphics file format. Graphs and drawings may be saved in the STATISTICA system graphics file format (file name extension *.stg*). Use the options *Save* or *Save As...* in the *File* menu. Although other graphics formats are also supported, this format is recommended whenever you intend to use the graph again in the STATISTICA system or link it to other application documents using the Windows OLE conventions. Unlike the other formats (see the next paragraph), the STATISTICA system

format stores not only the graphical representation of the picture but also the *Graph Data Editor* (see below) containing all data which are represented in the graph, all analytic options (fitted equations, ellipses, etc.) and other settings allowing you to continue the graphical data analysis at a later time. This format is also most appropriate if the current graph or drawing is later to be linked to or embedded into another STATISTICA graph. Graphs saved in this format can also be printed in batch using the *Print Files...* facility in the pull-down menu *File* (see page 101).

Bitmap and Metafile graphics format. If the graph to be saved is to be used by an application which does not support the STATISTICA graphics file format and does not support OLE, use the *Save Metafile...* or *Save Bitmap...* options (in the *File* menu) to store the current graph in the Windows metafile (file name extension *.wmf*) or Windows device-independent bitmap format (file name extension *.bmp*), respectively. Those formats (described briefly in the next two paragraphs) do not offer the advantages of customizability offered by the STATISTICA format (see above), however, they are compatible with all applications which support the Windows graphics file formats.

What is the Windows Metafile graphics format?

The *Metafile* format, also referred to as *Picture* (one of two standard Windows graphics formats used in Clipboard and disk file representations of graphs; file name extension *.wmf*) stores a picture as a set of descriptions or definitions of all components of the graph and their attributes (e.g., segments of lines, colors and patterns of those lines, specific fill patterns, text and text attributes, etc.).

Therefore, as compared to bitmaps (another standard Windows graphics format, see below), metafiles offer more flexible options for non-OLE modification and customization in other Windows applications.

For example, when you open a metafile in the Microsoft Draw program, you can "disassemble" the graph, select and modify individual lines, fill patterns, colors, edit text and change its attributes, etc.

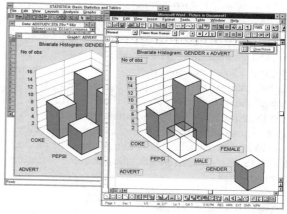

Note, however, that not all Windows applications support the complete set of metafile graphics features and attributes supported and used by STATISTICA, thus some aspects of STATISTICA graphs (saved as metafiles) will look different when they are opened in such applications (e.g., rotated and transformed fonts may appear unrotated). For best results, copy STATISTICA graphs to other applications using the OLE conventions which allow you to invoke STATISTICA to customize or modify STATISTICA graphs pasted into documents of other applications.

What is the *Bitmap* graphics format?

The *Bitmap* format (one of two standard Windows graphics formats used in Clipboard and disk file representations of graphs; file name extension *.bmp*) is similar to another standard Windows graph format--metafile (see above), in that it stores only the representation of the picture (and not the data which are plotted or any information about the analytic properties or settings used to produce the graph).

However, unlike the metafile format, the bitmap format stores only a "passive" representation of pixels

which form the graph. This representation is thus less customizable than *metafiles* which store dynamic representations of all individual graph components, thus allowing selective modifications of lines, text, etc., in other Windows applications.

Bitmaps can be opened by other Windows applications, but the customization or editing options of such graph representations will be limited (typically to operations on pixels, such as stretching and shrinking, cutting and pasting, and drawing "over" the graph). As mentioned before, for best results, copy STATISTICA graphs to other applications using the OLE conventions which allow you to invoke STATISTICA to customize or modify STATISTICA graphs pasted into documents of other applications.

What is the *Native* STATISTICA graphics format?

Unlike other graphics formats such as metafiles and bitmaps, the native STATISTICA graphics file format (file name extension *.stg) not only stores the "image" of the current graph but also all information necessary to continue graph customization or graphical data analysis (including all data represented in the graph, fitted equations, embedded graphs and artwork, links to graphs and artwork, etc.). Graphs stored in this format can be opened later (in any module of STATISTICA) allowing you to continue the graphical data analysis or graph customization (e.g., fit equations, add or merge new data series, etc.). Graphs saved in this format can also be printed in batch using the *Print Files...* facility in the pull-down menu *File* (see page 101). They can also be dynamically linked to documents of other Windows applications using the OLE conventions.

How to stop drawing or redrawing a graph:

Press any key or click the mouse anywhere on the screen. If the redrawing is related to some smoothing

or function-fitting calculations and the progress bar is displayed, then press the *Cancel* button on the progress bar (see the next topic).

How to stop function-fitting calculations:

Press any key, click the mouse anywhere on the screen, or (if the progress bar with the timer is displayed on the status bar) press the *Cancel* button located at the end of the progress bar. If the interruption of processing will involve losing some calculations that have already been performed, STATISTICA will ask you for confirmation before the processing is aborted.

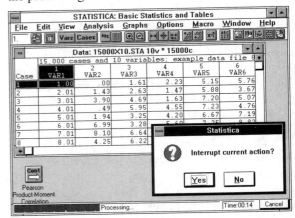

If you answer *No*, then the processing will resume. Note that STATISTICA supports multitasking, thus you can switch to some other application (including other modules of STATISTICA) and let the time-consuming process be completed in the background.

How to resume an interrupted redrawing of a graph:

Redrawing of an interrupted ("frozen") graph can be resumed either by pressing *OK* in any of the graph customization dialogs (see the pull-down menu *Layouts* or click the right-mouse-button anywhere on

the graph) or by touching the graph frame with the mouse as if you intended to resize the graph window.

Selecting the option *Restore Defaults* in the graph pull-down menu *View* will have the same effect but the graph will be redrawn in its default graph-window arrangement (i.e., using the default proportions, size in the window, and margins settings).

What is the difference between a *graph* and a *plot*?

Each plot represents a single "series" of data. All but the most simple *graphs* in STATISTICA contain more than one *plot* of data.

In other words, in STATISTICA, the term *graph* applies to a complete graphical representation of (one or more) "series" of data, that is, to the entire "picture," which can be saved as a graphics document (by default, as a STATISTICA graphics file, file name extension *.stg, see page 114).

There are many ways in which plots can be "put together" to form a graph, and depending on their *type*, some plots may require more than one sequence of values.

For example, at least three coordinated sequences of values are necessary to create a whisker plot: *X*-values, *Y1*-values (lower endpoints of whiskers), and *Y2*-values (upper endpoints of whiskers), as shown in the *Graph Data Editor*, below.

Graph Data: Distribution of MEASUR2 by MEASUR9 (ADSTUDY							
Distribution of MEASUR2 by MEASUR9 (ADSTUDY.STA 25v*50c)							
	Min-Max Min-Max X			25%-75% Min-Max X			Median value Scatterplot
	X	Y1	Y2	X	Y1	Y2	X	Y
1	1.00	1.00	9.00	1.00	1.00	6.00	1.00	4.00
2	2.00	1.00	8.00	2.00	1.00	7.00	2.00	6.00
3	3.00	4.00	9.00	3.00	4.00	8.00	3.00	8.00
4	4.00	4.00	6.00	4.00			4.00	4.50
5	5.00	3.00	9.00	5.00			5.00	7.00
6	6.00	0.00	8.00	6.00			6.00	4.50
7	7.00	2.00	6.00	7.00	2.00	6.00	7.00	5.00
8	8.00	0.00	9.00	8.00			8.00	5.50
9	9.00	0.00	3.00	9.00			9.00	1.50
10	10.00	0.00	8.00	10.00	0.00	4.50	10.00	2.00
11								

(Flying menu: Add Plot / Add Rows / Plot Layout / General Layout / Cut Ctrl+X / Copy Ctrl+C / Paste Ctrl+V / Clear Del)

Plots in the *Graph Data Editor*. One *Graph Data Editor* window (shown above, see also the next

topic for an overview) contains all data represented in a graph. In other words, it contains data for all plots in a single graph, and each plot is represented in the *Editor* by one column (typically a double- or triple-column).

The same general principle of "graphs consisting of plots," where each plot is represented by a custom-formatted column in the *Graph Data Editor* (see the next paragraph) applies to all types of graphs in STATISTICA (2D, 3D, and nD).

Customizing the layout of a graph (the *General Layout* dialog). The layout of a *graph* contains all those features and attributes which apply to the entire graph and are common to all plots. They include such features as titles, gridlines, global colors (backgrounds, etc.), scaling, axis labels, or categorization labels. They can be adjusted in the *General Layout* dialog (see page 118) accessible from the pull-down menu *Layouts*, or via flying menus (called by clicking the right-mouse-button on the graph or the *Graph Data Editor*, see below).

Customizing the layout of a plot (the *Plot Layout* dialog). On the other hand, the layout of a *plot* contains patterns, sizes, and all other specifications which apply to the graphical representation of only one series of data. They can be customized in the *Plot Layout* dialog (see page 119) accessible from the pull-down menu *Layouts*, via flying menus (called by clicking the right-mouse-button on the graph or the *Graph Data Editor*), or by clicking on the respective column of the *Graph Data Editor* (see the next topic).

What is the *Graph Data Editor*?

Access to all graph data. In STATISTICA, all values represented in every graph can be reviewed and edited directly. In other words, regardless of whether a graph represents raw data from the data spreadsheet, parts of a Scrollsheet output, or a set of calculated or derived scores (e.g., in a probability

plot), these values are always accessible along with the graph via the internal *Graph Data Editor*.

There is one such *Editor* associated with each graph and managed as a "child window" of the graph (which means that the *Editor* window will close when the graph is closed). The *Editor* is organized into column-segments representing individual plots (i.e., series of data, see the next topic) from the current graph.

Data: ADSTUDY.STA 25v * 50c Advertising Effectiveness Study.								
MEASUR1 Scatterplot		MEASUR2 Bar X		MEASUR3 Line Plot		MEASUR4 Min-Max Y		
X	Y	X	Y	X	Y	X	Y1	Y2
1	1.00	9.00	1.00	1.00	1.00	6.00	1.00	8.00	8.00
2	2.00	6.00	2.00	7.00	2.00	1.00	2.00	8.00	8.00
3	3.00	9.00	3.00	8.00	3.00	2.00	3.00	9.00	9.00
4	4.00	7.00	4.00	9.00	4.00	0.00	4.00	5.00	5.00
5	5.00	7.00	5.00	1.00	5.00	6.00	5.00	2.00	2.00
6	6.00	6.00	6.00	0.00	6.00	0.00	6.00	8.00	8.00
7	7.00	7.00	7.00	4.00	7.00	3.00	7.00	2.00	2.00
8	8.00	9.00	8.00	9.00	8.00	2.00	8.00	6.00	6.00
9	9.00	7.00	9.00	8.00	9.00	2.00	9.00	3.00	3.00
10	10.00	6.00	10.00	6.00	10.00	2.00	10.00	8.00	8.00
11	11.00	4.00	11.00	6.00	11.00	6.00	11.00	5.00	5.00
12	12.00	7.00	12.00	3.00	12.00	3.00	12.00	7.00	7.00

(flying menu at right: Add Plot / Add Rows / Plot Layout / General Layout / Cut Ctrl+X / Copy Ctrl+C / Paste Ctrl+V / Clear Del)

Columns representing individual *plots*.
In *mixed-type* graphs, each column-segment may represent a different type of plot (e.g., line plot, scatterplot), and those respective types are marked by icons in the column name areas of the *Editor*. The column-segments may consist of single-, double-, triple-, or quadruple-columns of values (depending on the type of the respective graph, see the previous topic). The legend of each plot is displayed in the header of the respective column (next to the icon representing the type of plot). Double-clicking on that column header will bring up the *Plot Layout* dialog, allowing you to edit the legend as well as adjust all other features and characteristics of the plot (patterns, fitted functions, etc., see page 119).

Data management options in the *Graph Data Editor*.
The contents of the *Editor* can be expanded (see the options *Add Plot* and *Add Rows* in the *Editor* pull-down menu *Edit*, or the flying menu accessible by clicking the right-mouse-button on the *Graph Data Editor*), combined with other data, or saved in tab-delimited data files, etc. (for more information, press *F1* in the *Editor*). When you save the graph,

the complete contents of the *Editor* are also stored in the graphics file, so that later you can continue interactive data analyses (e.g., brushing, see the next button).

Toolbar in the *Graph Data Editor*.
The toolbar buttons in the *Graph Data Editor* offer the standard data formatting and editing facilities, described before in the sections on the spreadsheet (see page 33) and Scrollsheet (see page 44) toolbars. In addition, it includes two buttons which initiate redrawing of the current graph: *Redraw* and *Exit+Redraw* (the latter closes the *Editor*), and the *P/L* and *G/L* buttons providing quick access to the two main graph customization dialogs: *Plot Layout* (see page 119), and *General Layout* (see page 118), respectively.

Marked values in the *Graph Data Editor*.
The *mark/un-mark* button (see the Scrollsheet button number 9, page 45) can be used to mark cells like in every other Scrollsheet. However, in the *Graph Data Editor* it has an additional function. In the default configuration, the marked values are temporarily eliminated from the graph (this is usually done by using the *Brushing* tool on the graph, see the graph toolbar button number 4, page 53). Until it is un-marked (by clicking on the button when the marked cell is highlighted), the marked data point is not displayed in the graph and, most importantly, it is ignored when functions are fitted to the data set. This interpretation of marked values in the *Editor* can be changed by de-selecting the *Ignore Marked Values* option in the pull-down menu *View*; when that option is de-selected, then both marked and un-marked points are plotted and included in fitting.

How to add a new *Plot* to an existing *Graph*:

Use the *Add Plot* option in the graph pull-down menu *Layouts* (or the flying menu accessible by clicking the right-mouse-button on the *Graph Data Editor*). A subsequent dialog will allow you to specify the plot to be added. A new column (or a double-, or triple-

column, depending on the plot type that you requested) will be added to the *Graph Data Editor* (see the previous topic) making room for data to be represented in that new plot. You can enter the data, paste them, or merge them from another graph.

How to customize STATISTICA graphs:

Customization *before* vs. *after* displaying a default graph.

All graph customization facilities in STATISTICA are available when a graph window is active (thus, after a graph has been shown). Usually, graphs appear on the screen instantaneously, and typically, it is preferable to first see the default appearance of the graph before proceeding with any customizations. However, in the rare cases when producing a graph takes more time (e.g., in case of complex multi-graphs or graphs based on very large data sets), you can also make the customization before the drawing of the default graph is completed. Specifically, you can always interrupt the drawing with a single click (press any key or click the mouse anywhere on the screen). Then, you can access some customization tools or facilities and resume redrawing after making the desired adjustments.

There are two major types of graph customizations:

- adding/editing custom graphic objects, and

- customizing the structural components of the graph.

Adding/editing custom graphic objects.

The tools to add and edit custom graphic objects to the current graph (such as drawing, managing and customizing objects, pasting, embedding, linking, etc.) can be accessed from the graphics toolbar. They are described in the section on the *Graphics Toolbar*, earlier in this manual (see page 52). Those options are also accessible via the keyboard (from the graph pull-down menu *Edit*), and many of them can also be accessed from the flying menus accessible by clicking on specific parts of the graph with the right-mouse-button (see the illustration below).

Customizing the structural components of the graph.

Almost all facilities to change the structural properties of graphs (such as proportions, scales, patterns, features of individual plots, etc.) can be accessed from two types of dialogs: *General Layout* and *Plot Layout*. They are described in the next two topics. These two types of dialogs can be accessed from the graph pull-down menu *Layouts*.

Using the right-mouse-button (flying menus in graphs).

However, the easiest way to access the two main types of customization dialogs (as well as all other customization facilities) is to use the flying menus accessible by clicking on the graph with the right-mouse-button. Using the flying menus is also often faster because they provide shortcuts allowing you to directly access the nested (i.e., "second-" or "third-level") dialogs controlling the attributes of specific graph components while bypassing the *General Layout* and *Plot Layout* dialogs.

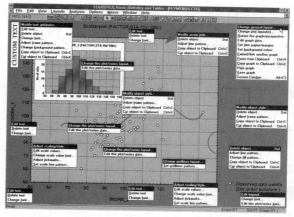

One of the graph flying menus has a different status than others. Specifically, unlike all other flying menus which are associated with specific objects, the "main" (or "background") flying menu (shown below) accessible by pressing the right-mouse-button anywhere outside the graph axes contains global graph customization and multi-graphics management options.

StatSoft™

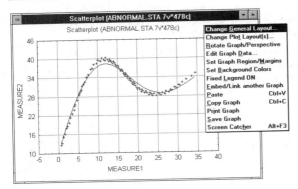

Using the left-mouse-button (direct access to customization dialogs).

Another mouse-based shortcut to access customization facilities for specific elements of the graph is to double-click on the specific graph object or component (using the left-mouse-button). If the element you have selected this way is one of the structural components of the graph (such as a scale, point marker, or a title), then the dialog which is most-commonly used to customize that type of the object will automatically open.

Options accessible by double-clicking on an object with the left-mouse-button vs. options accessible from the flying menus (clicking the right-mouse-button).

As mentioned before, by pointing with the right-mouse-button to an object, a list of customization dialogs and options applying to that object will be displayed in a flying menu. On the other hand, double-clicking using the left button opens directly the dialog most-commonly used, or the global dialog which applies to the object. Therefore, double-clicking with the left button saves you one step whenever you are accessing the most-commonly used option.

Accessing the *General Layout* dialog.

The same principle also applies to calling the *General Layout* dialog (see the next topic): to access it, simply double-click on the empty graph space outside the graph axes. Alternatively, you can select it from the "main" flying menu accessible by clicking with the right-mouse-button on the empty graph space outside the graph axes.

Customization of custom graphic objects (drawings, embedded objects).

The general principles of selecting objects by mouse and accessing their customization facilities (summarized in the two previous paragraphs) also apply to all custom graphic objects, such as drawings, arrows, and embedded objects. The graphics toolbar buttons can also be used to access most of those customization facilities. The section on the graphics toolbar (page 52) contains the relevant information. For example, the buttons can be used to change the dynamic vs. fixed coordinates of objects, their patterns, sizes and colors, properties of predefined objects (such as arrows or error bars), or foreign objects (e.g., pasted, linked, or embedded artwork).

Margins, graph proportions, plot area, zooming.

These global graph attributes can be adjusted by using the respective buttons on the graphics toolbar (see buttons number 5 through 9, pages 54-56); these options are also available on the graph pull-down menu *View*.

What is the *General Layout* dialog?

The *General Layout* dialog is one of two main graph customization dialogs (the other is the *Plot Layout* dialog, see the next topic).

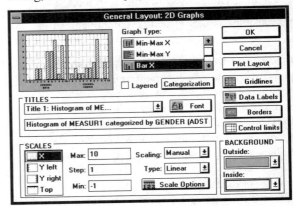

The *General Layout* dialog contains options to control and customize all those features and attributes

StatSoft™

which apply to the entire graph and are common to all component plots in the graph (see the section on differences between *graphs* and *plots*, page 115). They include such features as titles, gridlines, global colors (backgrounds, etc.), scaling, axis labels, or categorization labels.

How to access the *General Layout* dialog for the current graph. The *General Layout* dialog is accessible from the pull-down menu *Layouts*, as well as via flying menus (which can be called by clicking the right-mouse-button on the graph; it is the first option in the "main" flying menu, accessible when you click the right-mouse-button on the empty area outside the graph axes). However, the quickest way to access it is to double-click (left-mouse-button) on the empty area outside the graph axes.

Mixed-type graphs. As mentioned before, a graph may consist of plots of different types (see *graphs* vs. *plots*, page 115). Note, however, that one of the controls in the *General Layout* dialog allows you to change the *type* of graph (see the list box *Graph Type* with graph-type icons). This graph type control is set to a specific type only if all plots comprising the graph are of the same type. Otherwise, it is set to *Mixed*, which means that different plots are of different types. By changing the *Mixed* setting in this control to a single specific *type*, all component plots will be changed to this particular type.

Different formats of the *Plot Layout* dialogs. The format of the *Plot Layout* dialogs is somewhat different for each of the five main categories of graphs which can be produced in STATISTICA (see the next topic).

What is the *Plot Layout* dialog?

The *Plot Layout* dialog is one of two main graph customization dialogs (the other is the *General Layout* dialog, see the previous topic). It contains options to control and customize all those features and attributes which apply only to specific plots and

not necessarily to the entire graph (see the section on differences between *graphs* and *plots*, page 115). They include such features as type of plot, text of the legend, patterns, colors, and sizes of the plot representation, fitted function, confidence intervals or area settings for this plot, etc.

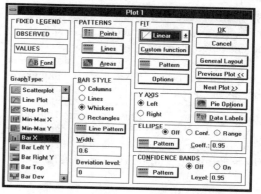

How to access the *Plot Layout* dialogs for specific plots. The *Plot Layout* dialogs (one for each of the plots in the current graph) are accessible:

• from a list of plots in the pull-down menu *Layouts*;

• by double-clicking on the respective plot column header (or using the flying menu) in the *Graph Data Editor* (see page 115); and

• directly from the graph via flying menus (if you click the right-mouse-button on any part of a specific plot, the flying menu will list its respective *Plot Layout* dialog as one of the options).

Different formats of the *Plot Layout* dialogs for different categories of graphs. Note that the formats of the *Plot Layout* dialogs are different for each of the five main categories of graphs which can be produced in STATISTICA (*2D Graphs, 3D Sequential Graphs, 3D XYZ Graphs, 3D Histograms,* and *nD Graphs and Icons*). If the category allows for only a single plot to be represented in a graph, then the *Plot Layout* customization settings are combined

with the *General Layout* settings into a single *General Layout and Plot Layout* dialog (e.g., in *3D Histograms*).

How to adjust the margins of a graph:

Margins within the graph area. Pressing the *graph area and margins* button on the graphics toolbar (see button number 7, page 55) allows you to adjust the space between the edge of the plotting area (i.e., the borders of the graph window) and any graph components or custom graphic objects.

Printout margins. The printout margins (the width of the distance between the edge of the paper and the beginning of the graph area) can be adjusted in the *Print Preview* dialog (pull-down menu *File*, see page 137).

How to change the proportions (aspect ratio) of a graph:

Use the graphics toolbar buttons number 5, 6, and 7 (see pages 54-55).

Normally, the first of these buttons (*MAR* mode -- *Maintain Aspect Ratio*) is depressed, thus the proportions are automatically maintained as you resize the graph. To change the proportions, press the second of these buttons which enables the free (non-proportional) graph window resizing mode. In this mode, the graph can be "stretched" or "squeezed" in one direction only, which changes the proportions between the X and Y coordinates of 2D displays and other relations between graph components. The modified proportions of the graph will be reflected in the printout (as can be examined using the *Print Preview* facility in the pull-down menu *File*). After achieving the desired proportions of the graph, it is advantageous to switch back to the *MAR* resizing mode (press the first of the three buttons), so that the

proportions are not inadvertently altered when resizing the graph.

Press the third of the three buttons to enable the *graph area and margins adjustment* mode. In this mode, like in the non-proportional graph window resizing mode (see above), the proportions of the entire graph area can now also be altered, however, it will not change the size or the aspect ratio (*X:Y*) of the graph itself but only add or cut some space of the surrounding graph area (see page 55).

How to customize the layout and format of an axis (min-max, scale-values, tickmarks, etc.):

Double-click on the respective axis to access the *Scale Options* dialog containing customization facilities for all features of the current axis (alternatively, you can adjust individual features of the axis by selecting them from the flying menu accessible by clicking the right-mouse button anywhere on the respective axis).

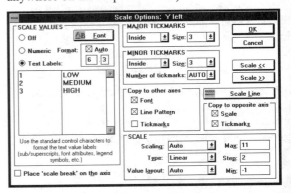

Note that the applicable features of the axis can be copied to other axes by setting the respective switches in the dialog (see above). You can copy the features either to the corresponding (i.e., the *opposite*) axis or all other axes. The main scaling features of each axis can also be adjusted in the *General Layout* dialog

(see page 118), from which you can also call the *Scale Options* dialogs for each scale.

How to replace numeric values on a scale with text value-labels:

In the *Scale Options* dialog (see the previous topic), set the *Scale Values* to *Text Labels*. Then, in the editable list box *Text Labels*, enter the appropriate numeric values (determining where the text labels are to be placed on the axis) and the corresponding text-value labels.

For example, if the values were entered as in the dialog shown in the previous topic, then the label *LOW* would be placed in the location of *1.00* on the axis, label *MEDIUM* in the location of *2.00*, etc.

What is the difference between the *Manual* and *Auto* (or *Manual/0* and *Auto/0*) scaling of a graph axis?

When the axis scaling is set to *Manual*, then the minimum, maximum, and step size for the axis are determined by the current values of the minimum, maximum, and step size (as entered in the respective fields of the *Scale Options* dialog, see the previous two topics). If it is set to *Auto* (i.e., automatic), then the program will automatically determine the scaling based on the range of values to be plotted.

The *Manual/0* and *Auto/0* settings work like *Manual* and *Auto* (respectively), except that the steps on the scale will be determined as if they always started from *0.0* and not the minimum of the scale (regardless of whether the value of *0.0* is actually included in the current range of the scale or not). The scaling mode for each axis can also be specified in the *General Layout* dialog (see page 118).

How to adjust the number of minor tickmarks (tickmarks between the scale values):

You can choose the number of minor tickmarks (as well as the default style and size of minor tickmarks) for each of the axes with the *Minor Tickmarks* options in the *Scale Options* dialog (see above). Double-click on the scale values of the axis in which you want the minor tickmarks to be displayed and select the desired number (from 1 to 15) of minor tickmarks. Selecting *Auto* will cause STATISTICA to select the optimum number of minor tickmarks. The default color and thickness of the tickmarks are determined by the current specifications of the respective scale line (see the *Scale Options* dialog, above).

How to place a scale (axis) break symbol:

You can place a 'break' in a graph axis in order to show that a break has occurred in the scale values (see below).

To do this, double-click on the scale values of the axis in which you want the break to occur. In the resulting *Scale Options* dialog, select the option *Place 'scale break' on the axis*. STATISTICA will place the break in the scale after you click *OK* in the *Scale Options* dialog.

How to customize the location and format of the legend:

Fixed vs. *movable* legends. Legends can be treated in two ways in STATISTICA graphs: either as fixed (unmovable) legends or movable legends. By default, when a graph is created, the legend is fixed (unmovable), which means that its position is automatically determined and the graph is moved to the left in the window to leave space for the legend (see below). You can make the graph legend movable so that you can reposition it in the graph and

StatSoft™

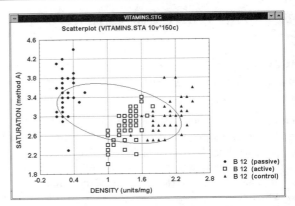

customize the text (e.g., add text beyond the 20 character limit, adjust line spacing and the distance between the legend symbols and the text, etc.) and other attributes of the graph legend by selecting the *Move Legend* option from the right-mouse-button flying menu (click on the fixed legend with the right-mouse-button, see below). When you select this option, the legend text will become like any other added text in the graph and you can edit the text (see page 57) or reposition the movable legend in the graph (click on it once and then drag it to the new position on the graph).

Fixed (unmovable) legends can be temporarily removed from the graph by selecting the *Fixed Graph Legend OFF* option from the right-mouse-button flying menu. The fixed legend(s) can then be placed back into the graph (in its default position) by selecting the *Fixed Graph Legend ON* option available from the "main" flying menu accessible by clicking the right-mouse-button anywhere in the empty space outside the graph region.

Superscripts, subscripts, and all other text format adjustments can be added to fixed legends using Control Characters (see page 124) in the appropriate *Plot Layout* dialog (see page 119), but (unlike the movable legend) fixed legends are limited in the number of characters that can be displayed in the legend (20).

The fixed legend font can be changed globally by double-clicking on the fixed legend or by selecting the *Change Font* option in the right-mouse-button flying menu.

Moving and reformatting the legend. By default, the legends are automatically formatted and placed in one of the fixed (typically most space-saving) locations of the graph area, as shown in the graph below.

For most graphs, the default legends are formatted as columns of items positioned on the right side of the graph; each legend symbol can be followed by up to two lines of text with up to 20 characters each, and the texts can be edited in the *Plot Layout* dialog for the respective plot (see page 119).

The *Move Legend* option to customize the location of the legend (accessible from the legend flying menu) will turn off that default legend mechanism and convert the legend into a block of custom text. This text will have the same status and properties as text pasted onto the graph or entered using the custom text tool (see button number 11 on the graphics toolbar, page 57). Thus, you can move the legend to any position on the graph and take advantage of all custom-text formatting facilities.

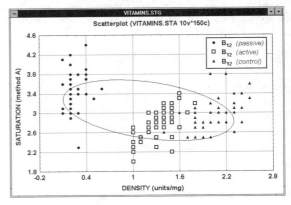

If you wish, you can include both fixed (unmovable) and movable legends in the same graph (see below). First, make the fixed legend movable by selecting the *Move Legend* option. Reposition this legend and then click on the graph background with the right-mouse-button and select the *Fixed Graph Legend ON* option from the flying menu. After you select this option, you will be asked if you want to remove (delete) the movable legend before placing the fixed legend in the graph. If you answer *No*, then the movable legend will remain and the fixed legend will be placed in its default position in the graph. If you answer *Yes*, then the movable legend will be deleted from the graph before the fixed legend is replaced.

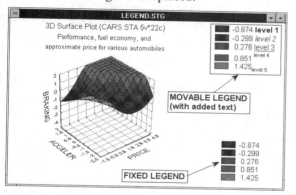

You can add a custom background, frame, place all items in one long line (by deleting the *line feed* characters from the end of each original line), or split the text into separate parts (select and cut a part of the legend, then paste it somewhere else).

What other types of legends are automatically created in graphs?

In addition to the standard *fixed* legend (which identifies patterns and colors used to mark individual plots in the graph), there are also other more specialized types of fixed legends. For example there are *contour* legends which identify the levels in surface or contour plots (see page 110), *icon* legends

which identify the assignment of components of the icons to specific variables (see page 134), or *selection* legends which identify the case selection conditions used to classify cases into multiple subsets shown on the graph (see page 134). All these fixed legends can be changed to movable legends following the same conventions outlined above. Also the *Fixed legend ON* option from the graph right-mouse-button flying menu will enable all fixed legends which were turned off.

How to add a title to a graph:

In every graph, there can be up to 11 lines of title text (5 on the top, 2 on the bottom, and 2 on each side), which are automatically positioned and centered.

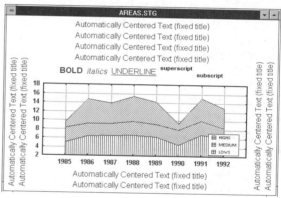

They can be edited in a scrollable dialog accessible by double-clicking on any title (you can access any one of the 11 lines of title in that dialog).

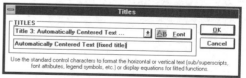

The titles can also be edited in the *General Layout* dialog (see page 118; see also the next topic).

Note that all text entry fields in STATISTICA graphs support the formatting control characters (see below),

thus titles can contain different text attributes (e.g., superscripts, italics), legend symbols, or text of any of the currently fitted equations.

For example, if you enter **@F[1]** in the title, then STATISTICA will replace this control character with the text of the current equation fitted to plot number 1 in the graph (see page 125).

How to place a graph title or a footnote in a fixed position:

Use the *Graphic Text Editor* (see page 57) to enter and position the title or footnote in the desired location.

If you intend for the text to stay in a particular place in the graph area regardless of the future changes to the graph scales or graph location (within the graph area), change the status of the object from the default *Dynamic* to *Fixed* (see page 52), which will keep the text in the absolute window coordinates regardless of the changes to the graph (e.g., in 5% of the window width and length from the upper left corner). See also the previous topic.

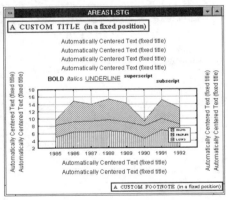

What are Control Characters?

Control Characters are specific characters that can be entered in graphic text (e.g., titles, legends, scale

values, added text, category values, category names) in order to customize the text.

If the text is entered via the *Graphic Text Editor* dialog (page 57), then specific customizations (e.g., attributes of text) can be entered by highlighting the respective part of the text and then pressing one of the mini-toolbar buttons. These buttons (accessible from the *Graphic Text Editor* dialog) are shown below:

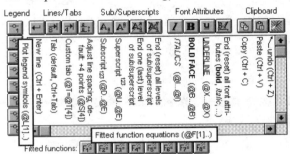

When you click on these buttons, STATISTICA will automatically insert the respective Control Characters into the text.

Both in the *Graphic Text Editor* window and in all other instances where the graphic text can be entered (e.g., in titles, legends, etc.), the Control Characters can by typed directly into the text. Some of the most commonly used Control Characters are listed below:

@B Bold font attribute (on/off)

@I Italic font attribute (on/off)

@X Underline font attribute (on/off)

@U Starts the superscript (one level)

@D Starts the subscript (one level)

@E Ends the super/subscript (one level)

@T Tab (default: 4 characters)

@S Changes the line spacing (default, i.e., when no parameters are specified: increase by 4 points)

@L Inserts the legend (pattern) symbol (default, i.e., when no parameters are specified: plot #1)

@F   Inserts the equation for a fitted function (default, i.e., when no parameters are specified: plot #1)

@N   Places the upper-bound value for the specified contour or surface plot level next to the respective contour line or surface pattern.

Control Characters that define a specific customization option always begin with an @ symbol which is followed by a letter designating the option, optionally with values for that option in brackets (e.g., **@T[4]** specifies a tab of four spaces). If you enter just the @ symbol and a letter without any value assigned to it, then the default value will be assigned (see the on-line *electronic manual* for a complete description of each of the control characters and their default values, where applicable). In most cases, placing the control code before the text will affect all of the text following that code.

For example, **@B** turns on/off the bold font style, therefore, the text entered as:

     This is **@B**BOLD**@B** style

will appear as:

     This is **BOLD** style

The control character for the legend pattern symbol for plot number 1 is **@L[1]**, and **@U** starts the superscript style and **@E** ends the superscript style, therefore, the text entered as:

     @L[1]   X**@U**2**@E** values

will appear as:

     ▨ X^2 values

(in the last example, the specific legend pattern symbol depends on the current plot number 1).

Please refer to the on-line *electronic manual* for more detailed explanations and examples of Control Characters.

How to format text (e.g., use italics, sub- and superscripts, etc.) in graphs:

If the text is entered into the *Graphic Text Editor* (see page 57), highlight the part of the text to be changed and press the respective mini-toolbar button (e.g., bold). If the text is entered outside the *Graphic Text Editor*, then use the Control Characters as explained in the previous topic. The same Control Characters (i.e., **@I**, **@D**, **@U**, etc.) can be used to format and customize all types of text in STATISTICA graphs (e.g., titles, value labels, category names and values, scale labels, custom text, etc.).

How to fit a function (line or surface) to data:

Access the *Plot Layout* dialog (see page 119) for the respective plot; then, select the desired type of function or smoothing procedure to be used from the list box *FIT* (note that for some 3D graphs the *Plot Layout* and *Graph Layout* dialogs are combined). You can adjust the fitting options (e.g., stiffness or optimization settings) and the pattern for the graphical representation of the fit by pressing the *Options* and/or *Pattern* buttons, respectively (they are located in the *FIT* area of the dialog). The pattern can also be adjusted by double-clicking on the fit line or surface in the graph. (See also the section *How to Fit a Custom-Defined Function to the Data*, below.)

How to display a specific equation for the fitted function (e.g., a polynomial function):

You can use the Control Characters for the fitted function in a specific title or in the *Graphic Text Editor* in order to place the fitted function in the graph. The Control Characters are **@F[plot number, subgraph number]** where you specify

StatSoft™

the desired plot number and optionally the subgraph number (for categorized graphs). For example, if you enter the control characters **@F[2]** into the fixed title of the graph, then STATISTICA will enter in that title position, the fitted function for the second plot in a multiple plot graph (i.e., a 2D line plot with 3 plots). If you enter the control characters **@F[1,3]** in a title, then STATISTICA will place in that title position the fitted function for the third subgraph in a categorized graph. For other options and details, see the on-line *electronic manual*.

Displaying the text of fitted function equations in *Stats Graphs*.

In *Stats Graphs* (available from the pull-down menu *Graphs*, see page 106), the display of the text of the fitted function equations can be requested by selecting the *Display Fitted Function (equations)* option in the *Options* dialog. (That dialog controls settings which are common for many types of *Stats Graphs* and it is accessible by pressing the *Options* button in every *Stats Graphs* definition dialog.)

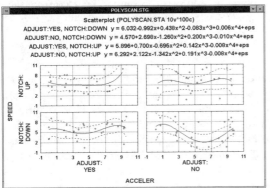

In all one-plot and non-categorized graphs where only one function is fitted, the text of the equation is displayed in the first available line of the fixed title. Depending on the number of equations to be displayed, also in categorized graphs, the equations can be displayed in the fixed titles of the graph (typically four lines are available if the custom *Job Title* or *Graph Title* options are not used, see the *Options* dialog). For example, in the graph above,

the text of four equations is displayed in the fixed title of the graph.

However, if more equations need to be displayed than the number of lines available in the fixed title, then STATISTICA will create a custom text object on the graph and place the equations there. Potentially, such lists of equations may be very long (e.g., include 256 equations), and thus the custom text object may be large and partially cover the graph. However, the location of the listing of functions can be adjusted (the list can be moved around and edited like any other custom text object, the font size can be reduced, etc.).

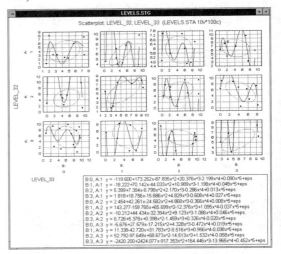

When the listing of functions is very long, it is recommended to add some space around the graph (see page 55) and place the text object there (as shown in the example above).

How to plot a custom-defined function:

First, access the *Plot Layout* dialog (see page 119) for the respective plot (e.g., use the graph pull-down menu *Layouts* or a flying menu; note that for some 3D graphs the *Plot Layout* and *Graph Layout* dialogs are combined). In the *Plot Layout* dialog, press the *Custom Function* button to access the custom-

equation editor and specify the equation to be plotted in the 2D or 3D graph.

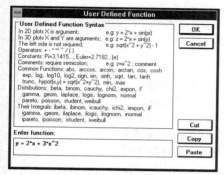

In addition to the standard math functions, a variety of functions representing distributions as well as their integrals (inverses) are supported and can be plotted (including *beta, binomial, Cauchy, Chi-square, exponential, F, gamma, geometric, Laplace, logistic, normal, log-normal, Pareto, Poisson, Student,* and *Weibull* distributions). Press *F1* to access comprehensive syntax description and examples in the *electronic manual*.

How to fit a custom-defined function to data:

The custom-function plotting facility (see the previous topic) accessible in the *Plot Layout* dialog (see page 119) will only plot the requested (custom-defined) functions and overlay them on the existing graph, but it will not fit these functions to the data. A selection of the most-commonly used, predefined functions which can be fitted to the data is available from the same dialog (e.g., *linear, logarithmic, exponential,* various *polynomial, distance-weighted least squares, spline,* and others); see the section *How to fit a function (line or surface) to data,* above. Comprehensive facilities to fit to data (and interactively plot in two or three dimensions) user-defined functions of practically unlimited complexity are provided in the *Nonlinear Estimation* module.

How to change the axis-proportions (aspect ratio) in 3D graphs:

Unlike 2D graphs, where changes to the aspect ratio require adjusting a relation between only two measures ($X{:}Y$, and thus can be accomplished by non-proportional graph window resizing, see page 54), the aspect ratio for 3D displays is defined by three parameters ($X{:}Y{:}Z$).

The non-proportional window resizing mode will not affect the axis proportions in 3D graphs, it will only result in adjustments of the margins of the plot area. In order to adjust the axis aspect ratio, press the *More Options...* button in the *General Layout* dialog (see page 118).

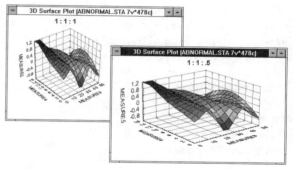

Use the *Axis Proportions* section of the *3D Graphs-/More Options* dialog to make the adjustments.

How to rotate a 3D graph:

Either use the *Rotation and Perspective* control button on the graphics toolbar to access the interactive rotation control facility (button number 30, see page 66), or press the *More Options...* button in the *General Layout* dialog (see page 118), to enter specific *viewpoint parameters* controlling the position of the imaginary viewpoint against the 3D object.

StatSoft™

How to adjust the perspective ("viewpoint") in a 3D graph:

Either use the *Rotation and Perspective* control button on the graphics toolbar to access the interactive perspective adjustment facility (button number 30, see page 66), or press the *More Options...* button in the *General Layout* dialog (see page 118), to enter specific *viewpoint parameters* controlling the position of the imaginary viewpoint against the 3D object.

How to review cross-sections of a 3D graph:

An *Animated stratification* option is accessible by pressing the respective button on the toolbars of all 3D sequential graphs (see button number 31, page 66). A dialog will appear on the top of the graph allowing you to control the display of consecutive "slices" of the display.

How to use the "X-ray" facility to explore layers of 3D graphs:

In addition to the animated stratification option (see the previous topic), in the default pointing mode (when the *Point Tool* is enabled; see button 10, page 57), you can selectively highlight individual plots in the graph by pressing the left-mouse-button anywhere on the selected plot.

For example, in sequential 3D plots, this option allows you to temporarily highlight complete series of data even if the respective plots are almost entirely covered by other plots (as if you were "X-raying" a plot). If the plot of interest is covered entirely, click on its legend to achieve the same result. This facility is also useful in examining other types of 2D and 3D graphs as it allows you to uncover invisible areas of specific plots or discriminate between different plots (e.g., in multiple scatterplots). In 3D histograms,

which belong to a "one-plot only" category of graphs (see *plot* vs. *graph*, page 115), the selection facility can also be useful to review the hidden layers of the graph because in those specific graphs (3D histograms), the tool is automatically set to highlight individual layers and not separate plots.

How to interactively review points which belong to specific plots in multiple scatterplots and other multiple graphs:

Identifying all points of a plot. In the (default) pointing mode (when the *Point Tool* is enabled; see button 10, page 57), click with the left-mouse-button on any point that belongs to the specific plot and all points of that plot will become highlighted. They will stay highlighted for as long as you keep the mouse-button pressed. If there are many plots in the graph, and their respective point markers are small and difficult to identify, then you can click on the legend (with the left-mouse-button). This will also highlight all points that belong to the respective plot.

Identifying individual points of a plot. If you need to identify values of specific points in the graph, use the *Brushing Tool* (see page 53).

What are the Display Filters?

This facility, accessible from the graph pull-down menu *View*, allows you to control the degree of "display filtering," that is, removal of overlapping points or text in the current graph.

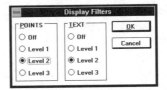

STATISTICA examines each point or text and does not draw the overlapping points or text within a

designated radius (determined by the *level* of filtering) in order to increase the readability of the graph and speed up the graph redrawing process.

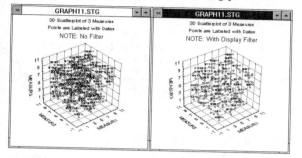

The higher the *level* setting, the larger the filtering radius, for example:

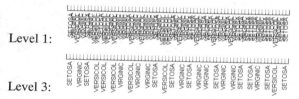

Level 1:

Level 3:

In order to disable filtering, set the *Display Filters* to *Off*.

Dense scale values, point markers, or value labels are not displayed in the graph. How do I adjust the display to see them all?

The display of overlapping items is suppressed by the *Display Filters* facility designed to increase the readability of the graph and speed up the graph redrawing process. In order to see all (overlapping) items, turn off the *Display Filters* (see the previous topic).

How to define a custom palette for a surface plot:

Double-click on the surface of the graph to access the *3D Graphs/More Options* dialog (this dialog is also accessible by pressing the *More Options...* button in the *General Layout* dialog, see page 118). Then, press the *Edit Palette* button to bring up the *Edit Palette* dialog.

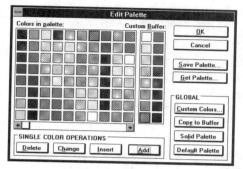

Now, you can build a custom palette by inserting, deleting, adding, and replacing colors. As you build the palette, you can press the *Custom Colors* button to define custom colors whenever necessary.

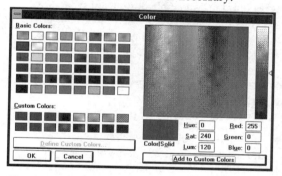

The *Edit Palette* dialog can also be used to save and retrieve palettes to/from disk files (the default file name extension for palette files is *.pal).

How to place one STATISTICA graph into another:

Pasting one graph in another. The easiest way to place one graph into another is to copy a graph displayed in one window (press *Ctrl+C*, press the toolbar button *Copy*, or use option *Copy graph to Clipboard* in the "main" flying menu accessible by

clicking the right-mouse-button anywhere on the outside of the graph axes). Then, move to the target graph window and paste it there (press *Ctrl+V*, press the toolbar button *Paste*, or use the flying menu). The pasted graph will appear in the upper-left corner of the target graph. Now, you can move or resize it like every other custom graphic object.

You can also change the properties of the pasted object by selecting the *Object Style* option from its respective flying menu (click on an object with the right-mouse-button). You can also edit the embedded object by double-clicking on it (following the standard OLE conventions). Refer to page 65 for more information on graph and artwork pasting and the relevant options available in STATISTICA.

Linking and embedding. Graphs and artwork saved into disk files can also be dynamically linked or statically embedded in the current graph by using the integrated linking and embedding facility, accessible by pressing the respective graph toolbar button (see page 61 for a description of these operations and differences between linking and embedding).

How to place a foreign graph or artwork in a STATISTICA graph:

The Clipboard-based as well as linking and embedding operations listed in the previous topic apply to all Windows-compatible graphs and artwork (linking and embedding operations support graphs and artwork saved into bitmap-format files, Windows graphics metafiles, and STATISTICA format graph files; for more information, refer to page 61).

How to place text (e.g., reports, tables, etc.) in a STATISTICA graph:

Even large portions of text (e.g., a report several pages long) can be pasted into STATISTICA graphs using the Clipboard operations mentioned in the previous two topics (for more information, see page

65). The text can then be edited and customized (within STATISTICA graphs) using the *Graphic Text Editor* (see page 57).

Both the Clipboard-based as well as linking and embedding operations listed in the previous topic apply to all Windows-compatible graphs and artwork (linking and embedding operations support graphs and artwork saved into bitmap-format files, Windows graphics metafiles, and STATISTICA format graph files; for more information, refer to page 61).

How to copy an entire STATISTICA graph to the Clipboard:

Make sure that the window containing the graph to be copied is active, then press *Ctrl+C*. Alternatively, you can press the toolbar button *Copy*, or select the option *Copy graph to Clipboard* in the "main" flying menu accessible by clicking the right-mouse-button anywhere on the outside of the graph axes. For more information, see page 65.

STATISTICA graphs can be pasted to other application documents (e.g., word processor documents, spreadsheets) either as "passive" objects (using the regular *Paste* or *Ctrl+V* command in the other application) or as active objects (via OLE). If STATISTICA graphs are pasted to other applications via Windows OLE conventions, they maintain their relation to STATISTICA and thus can be interactively edited from within the other application.

How to copy a selected part of a STATISTICA graph to the Clipboard:

Copying an object. Select a graphic object to be copied by clicking on it (be sure that you are in the default pointing mode, i.e., the *Point Tool* button on the toolbar is pressed, see page 57). Graphic objects are all objects you have created on the screen, such as a custom text, a segment of a drawing, or an embedded graph or artwork). When the object is

selected (highlighted), press *Ctrl+C*. Alternatively, you can press the toolbar *Copy* button. (For information on supported Clipboard formats, see page 65.)

Copying a rectangular section of the graph.

Enable the *Screen Catcher* tool by pressing *Alt+F3* (or selecting it from the pull-down menu *Edit* or the "main" flying menu options accessible by clicking the right-mouse-button anywhere on the outside of the graph axes). The cursor will change to a small circle with a cross hair; place the cross hair in the upper left corner of the area to be copied, then drag it to the lower right corner (a rectangle will indicate the exact area which you are selecting). When you release the mouse button, the selected area will be automatically copied to the Clipboard in the bitmap format (there is no need to press the *Copy* button). Note that the *Catcher* can be used to copy any rectangular part of the screen, not only in the graph window from which it was called but any part of the screen (even including parts that belong to other applications).

When selecting the area to be captured, you can rotate by 180°, and/or reverse (produce a mirror image of) the area captured to the Clipboard by choosing one of four directions of dragging the mouse.

AB AB
AB ∀B
AB ∀B
AB ∀B

The four examples above illustrate how the area captured with the *Screen Catcher* facility will be rotated (which can be achieved by dragging the mouse in different directions over the area to be captured) and displayed in the Clipboard.

What is the Screen Catcher?

The *Screen Catcher* is a STATISTICA utility which can be used to copy any part of the screen to the

Clipboard (for details, see the second part of the previous topic).

How to create a "blank" graph (space for drawings or artwork to be pasted or linked/embedded):

Select the *Blank Graph* option from either the spreadsheet or Scrollsheet *Graphs* pull-down menus in order to open a blank graph. Here, you can add new or existing graph objects (e.g., added text, embedded or linked objects, arrows, free-hand drawings, previously saved graphs, etc.). The *Alignment Grid* (an 8x8 grid; accessible from the *Graphics* window pull-down menu *View*) or the dynamically updated cursor coordinates (see the *Show Field*, page 52) can be used to aid in the placement and alignment of the graph objects in the blank graph.

Blank graphs can be created in the default or printer page proportions. When you select the *Default Proportion* option, the proportions of the blank graph window will follow the default graph window properties (i.e., it will not necessarily be the same as the current printer/page proportions, e.g., portrait/landscape, margins, etc.). The graph proportion can later be adjusted via the *Use Print Proportion* option from the *View* pull-down menu (so that the graph will fill the physical size of the printed page) or the *Change Proportions* option in the *View* pull-down menu.

Selecting the *Printer Page Proportions* option will open a blank graph window which is proportional to the current printer page proportions, as specified in the *Print Preview*, *Margins*, and *Printer Setup* dialogs (e.g., portrait or landscape). The blank graph proportion will automatically be adjusted so that the graph will fill the physical size of the printed page. This is especially useful when pasting more than one graph into the blank graph (in order to place more than one graph on a page). The graph proportions

can later be adjusted to the default proportions via the *Restore Defaults* option in the *View* pull-down menu.

How to place multiple graphs on one page:

Start by creating a blank graph (see the previous topic), then paste, link, or embed the graphs or artwork and arrange them and resize as needed. All objects can be dragged or resized in the usual manner. Note that you can use the *Object Style* option from the flying menus of individual objects to adjust their resizing mode (maintain vs. change original proportions), redrawing mode (filled vs. transparent background) and other properties. Optionally, switch to the non-proportional graph window resizing mode (see page 54) to adjust the graph area proportions for the entire multiple graph window (e.g., instead of the default horizontal graph layout, you may resize the graph to achieve the portrait 11' x 8.5' proportions).

You may use the *Alignment Grid* option (from the graph pull-down menu *View*) or watch the exact cursor coordinates (in the *Show Field*, see page 52) to align the graphs. The *Print Preview* option (see page 137) can be used to adjust the printout margins and review the graph as it will appear when printed:

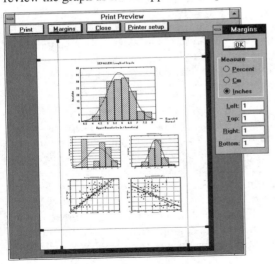

Note that alternatively, instead of starting with a blank graph, you can add extra space to an existing graph (see page 55), and then paste or link/embed new graphs in that space.

How to export a STATISTICA graph to another application:

Export via the Clipboard (and *Paste* or *Paste Special* via OLE). The quickest way to export a graph is to copy it to the Clipboard (see page 65) and then paste it into another application. STATISTICA native, Windows metafile (see page 113), and bitmap (see page 113) formats are created in the Clipboard and can be used in other applications.

STATISTICA graphs can be pasted to other application documents (e.g., word processor documents, spreadsheets) either as "passive" objects (using the regular *Paste* or *Ctrl+V* command in the other application) or as active objects (via OLE). If STATISTICA graphs are pasted to other applications via Windows OLE conventions, they maintain their relation to STATISTICA and thus can be interactively edited from within the other application.

Linking STATISTICA graph files via OLE. Graph files linked via OLE to other applications can also maintain their dynamic relations to the STATISTICA source files and thus they are automatically updated when the STATISTICA source files change.

Export to another file format. STATISTICA graphs can also be saved to other graphics file formats; use the *Save Metafile...* or *Save Bitmap...* options (in the *File* menu) to store the current graph in the Windows metafile (file name extension *.wmf) or Windows device-independent bitmap format (file name extension *.bmp), respectively.

StatSoft™

How to convert a graph file into a data file:

STATISTICA graphics files (file name extension *.stg*) can by imported as a "data" file using one of the data file import facilities provided in the *Data Management* module.

What are categorized graphs?

Categorized graphs are created by categorizing data into subsets and then displaying each of these subsets in a separate small component graph arranged in one display. For example, one graph may represent *male* subjects and one *female* subjects, or *high blood pressure females, low blood pressure females, high blood pressure males*, etc.

In STATISTICA, categorized graphs are:

- available in many output dialogs (they are automatically generated as part of output from all procedures which analyze groups or subsets of data, e.g., breakdowns, *t*-tests, ANOVA, discriminant function analysis, nonparametrics, and many others),

- accessible as part of the *Quick Stats Graphs* options in the flying menus in all Scrollsheets and spreadsheets, and

- accessible as part of *Stats Graphs* (from the pull-down menu *Graphs*) where a wide variety of user-defined methods to categorize data are available.

Refer to the next topic for a review of categorization methods available in STATISTICA.

How to define "categories" for categorized graphs:

If categorized graphs are requested from output dialogs of specific procedures which involve analyses of subsets of data, then they will automatically display the subsets which are currently analyzed (i.e., the subsets are already defined as part of the current analysis). On the other hand, the categorized *Stats Graphs* requested from the pull-down menu *Graphs* offer a variety of methods to specify subsets using one or two grouping variables. Also, custom-defined subset definitions can be used which can involve all variables in the current data set.

Specifically, categories can be defined by:

- Integer values of grouping variables (*Integer Mode*),

- Dividing grouping variables into a requested number of equal-length intervals (*# of Categories:*),

- Custom intervals (ranges) of grouping variables, defined by specific interval boundaries (*Boundaries:*),

- Specific values (i.e., codes) of grouping variables (*Codes:*), and

- User-defined "multiple-subset" definitions (*Multiple Subsets*) which can be entered as logical case selection conditions of virtually unlimited complexity (this categorization method may involve values of all variables in the current data file as shown below).

The following is a relatively complex example of a two-way categorized graph based on a mixed method of defining the subset (component) graphs. The two-way categorization means that the arrangement of the small (component) graphs in the display resembles a two-way table (crosstabulation) resulting from applying two different criteria of categorization.

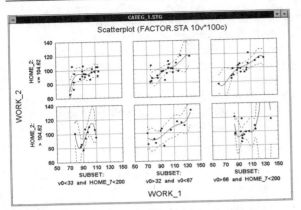

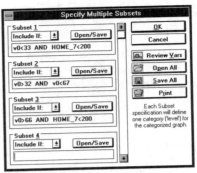

For example, in the graph shown above, the two rows of graphs represent categories defined based on values of variable *HOME_2* (cases where *HOME_2* is less than or equal to *104.62* and cases where it is greater than *104.62*). The three columns of graphs represent subsets of cases defined using specific "multiple subset" definitions based on values of variable number *0* (i.e., case numbers) and variable *HOME_7*. The following is the graph definition dialog where the above graph was defined.

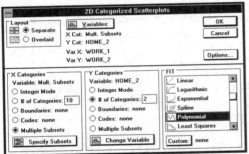

Specifically, variable *WORK_1* and *WORK_2* are plotted in each small graph (as variables *X* and *Y*, respectively). One of the two categorizations (*X Categories*, or "columns" of graphs) was defined as *Multiple Subsets* in a dialog which opens after pressing the *Specify Subsets* button:

The other of the two categorizations (*Y Categories*, or "rows" of graphs) was defined by a grouping variable (*HOME_2*), by dividing its range into two equal-length intervals, see the *# of Categories* field set to *2* in the graph definition dialog (which resulted in dividing the distribution of *HOME_2* into cases below or equal to, and above *104.62*, as can be seen in the above graph).

How to identify (in graphs) specific subsets of data:

Stats Graphs (accessible in the pull-down menu *Graphs*) offer facilities to define subsets of cases to be identified in graphs. User-defined "multiple-subset" definitions of such subsets can be entered as logical case selection conditions of virtually unlimited complexity using facilities identical to those illustrated in the previous topic.

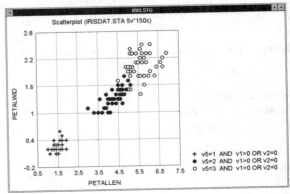

These subset identification facilities are supported in many types of *Stats Graphs*, including matrix plots:

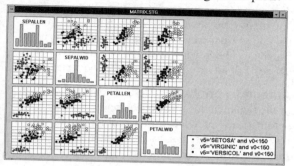

icon plots:

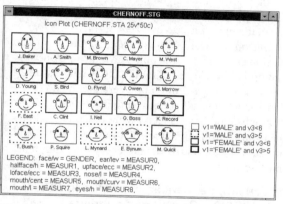

2D scatterplots, 3D scatterplots, 3D trace plots and other graphs.

How to display definitions of subsets which are too long to fit in the *Fixed* legend:

The length of *fixed* legends which display subset definitions is limited to 24 characters; if your subset definitions are longer, then instruct STATISTICA to place the text of definitions in a *movable* legend (which has the same status as custom text entered into the graph and thus its length is not limited, see page 121).

In the graph definition dialog for the respective graph (the one from which you select the variables to be displayed in the graph), access the *Stats Graphs: Options* dialog by pressing the *Options* button (this button is always located in the upper part of the dialog, below the buttons *OK* and *Cancel*). The *Stats Graphs: Options* dialog contains global settings which are common to most *Stats Graphs*. Select the option *Create long legends for mult. subset graphs*; the legend containing the subset definitions will now be created as custom text (of practically unlimited length), for example:

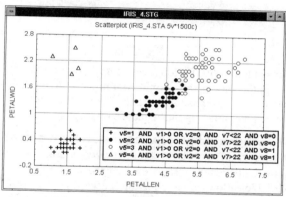

The initial position of such long legends may not be optimal, however, you can move it, reformat, reduce, place in fixed titles, etc. Note that all *fixed* legends can also be converted into movable legends (see page 121), however, the length of text which can be placed in *fixed* legends (at the point when the graph is created) is limited, therefore, if your subset definitions are long, it is recommended to create the initial legend as *moveable* (see above).

How to produce sequences of graphs from lists of variables:

Specifying lists of variables for *Stats Graphs*.
Most of the graph definition dialogs in *Stats Graphs* (accessible from the pull-down menu *Graphs*) allow you to select lists of variables in instances where a single variable is sufficient to define a graph. When

such a list of variables is specified, STATISTICA will cycle through the list and produce one graph for each variable (e.g., a histogram or a line plot).

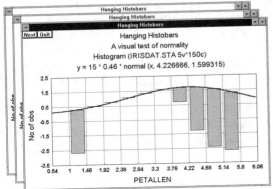

Pressing the *Next* button (see the upper-left corner of the graph shown above) will continue displaying the sequence of graphs; pressing the *Quit* button will interrupt displaying the sequence of graphs.

"Cascades" of graphs requested from output dialogs.

Most of the output (*Results*) dialogs in those statistical procedures which process lists of variables allow you to generate "cascades" of graphs for each (or each combination) of the variables in the current list. For example, such graphs can be produced from descriptive statistics, correlations, frequencies, crosstabulations, breakdowns, and other procedures:

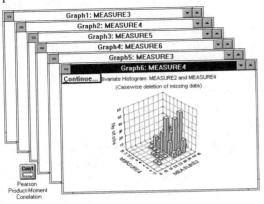

Pressing the *Continue* button (see the upper-left corner of the graph shown above) will continue displaying the sequences of graphs. Pressing the "floating" *Cont* (continue) button with the name of the dialog from which the sequence of graphs was called (see the lower-left corner of the display shown above) will interrupt displaying the sequence.

Automatic printouts.

Note that when using either of the two methods mentioned above, one can automatically produce printouts of all graphs displayed on the screen by enabling the *Automatically Print All Graphs* option in the *Page/Output Setup* dialog (see page 137). When, instead of reviewing the graphs on-screen, you need to quickly produce hard copies (e.g., printouts), then it is advantageous to select the option *Auto-Exit from Scrollsheets and Graphs* in the *STATISTICA Defaults: General* dialog (option *General...* in the pull-down menu *Options*). If that option is selected, STATISTICA will "internally" press the *Continue* button on every graph and Scrollsheet, thus allowing you to print long sequences of graphs (and Scrollsheets) without having to press the *Continue* button at the end of every "queue-full" of output windows (by default every third graph or third Scrollsheet).

Specifying sequences of graphs in *SCL* (STATISTICA Command Language).

Finally, multiple graphs can be generated in batch using *SCL* (the command language, see page 26). *SCL* is well-suited to "programming" sequences of specific tasks including graphs which can be automatically generated in long series.

Printing Graphs

How to print graphs:

The quickest method to print the current graph is to press the *Print* button on the graphics toolbar (see page 65), which is a shortcut method to print the graph following the default graph printout settings (or settings as they were last modified in the *Print Options*, dialog). If you need to modify any graph printout settings, use the *Print* option in the pull-down menu *File*. Unlike the *Print* button on the toolbar, using the menu option will not initiate the printing immediately, but will first display an intermediate dialog (*Print Options*) allowing you to adjust various printout and printer settings (see the next topic). Use the *Print Preview* option (pull-down menu *File*) to see how the graph will appear on the page and to adjust the margins.

Automatic printing. If you want STATISTICA to automatically print every graph which is displayed on the screen, select the *Automatically Print All Graphs* option in the *Page/Output Setup* dialog (accessible by double-clicking on the *Output* field on the status bar at the bottom of the STATISTICA window; see page 71). Each graph will be automatically printed without displaying any intermediate dialogs or asking you for confirmation. When this automatic graph printing facility is used with analyses which generate large numbers of graphs (e.g., cascades of 3D histograms for every "slice" of a multi-way table), then it is advantageous to select the *Auto-Exit from Scrollsheets and Graphs* option (see page 103) in the *Defaults: General* dialog (select the option *General...* in the pull-down menu *Options*). If that option is selected, STATISTICA will "internally" press the *Continue* button on every graph and Scrollsheet, thus allowing you to print long sequences of graphs without waiting for you to press the *Continue* button at the end of every "queue-full" of graphs. (See also

the batch printing facilities offered in the *Graphics* module of STATISTICA.)

Batch printing. There is also a batch printing facility which can be used to print previously-saved graphs. It is available by selecting the *Print Files...* option from the pull-down menu *File*, see page 101.

How to modify the graph printout settings (margins, resolution, dithering):

Print Preview. If you wish to see the graph as it will appear on the page, or modify the size of the print area and the margins of the printout, use the *Print Preview* facility accessible in the pull-down menu *File*.

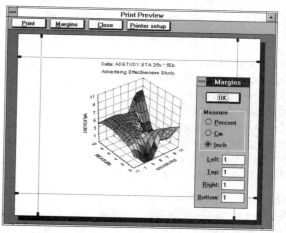

The *Print Preview* window is resizable, thus you can see details of the graph as they will appear on the printout. The margins can be adjusted (after pressing the *Margins* button) by dragging the margin lines or entering specific printout size measurements (in inches, centimeters, or percentages).

Graph printout settings. If you need to modify any graph printout settings, use the *Print* option in the pull-down menu *File*. Unlike the *Print* button on the toolbar (see page 65), using this option will not

initiate the printing immediately, but will first display an intermediate dialog (*Print Options*) allowing you to adjust various printout and printer settings.

Print Graph dialog:

> Printer: Default Printer (IBM LaserPrinter 4029 PS39 on LPT1:)
> OK
> Cancel
> Setup...
> ☐ Use dithered color to fill background
> ☐ Use dithered color for solid lines
> Min. line thickness (printer pixels): 1
> Help
> Print Quality: 600 dpi   Copies: 1
> ☐ Print to File
> Note: In order to print non-transparent objects, some printer drivers require that the driver option 'Print TrueType as Graphics' be enabled.

Note that some printer drivers support some of the advanced printer control features used by STATISTICA (e.g., background shading or text rotation) only when they are set to a higher resolution (e.g., higher than 150 DPI) and/or when they are set to print fonts as graphics (see the next topic for more information).

Do all printer drivers support rotated fonts? (Some rotated fonts appear horizontal on the printout even though they are properly rotated on the screen and in the *Print Preview* mode.)

Most properly configured printers supported by Windows can properly handle rotated fonts, however, some printer drivers support some of the advanced printer control features used by STATISTICA only when they are set to a higher resolution (e.g., higher than 150 DPI) and/or when they are set to print fonts as graphics. If you encounter problems (e.g., rotated text is printed as unrotated or "uncovered" text which was supposed to be covered), first try to enable the *Print TrueType as Graphics* option in the *Setup/Options* dialog of the *Printer Setup...* (pull-down menu *File*). If this does not help, set the printer to a higher resolution (e.g., change 150 DPI to 300 DPI). Note also that in Windows 3.1, one can

simultaneously maintain different printer settings (e.g., resolution, page orientation, etc.) for different applications. Moreover, STATISTICA allows you to maintain different printer settings for text reports and graphics (e.g., you can print text in portrait mode at 150 DPI and graphics in landscape mode at 300 DPI).

Do all printers support the non-transparent overlaying of graphic objects?

Most properly configured printers supported by Windows can properly handle printing of non-transparent overlays used in STATISTICA graphs; see the previous topic for advice on how to configure the printer driver.

How to control the minimum line thickness in graph printouts:

This setting can be adjusted in the *Print Options* dialog (see the first topic in this section), and the minimum line thickness setting entered there will override any smaller line thickness settings specified for individual graph components (see page 62).

How to make the light graph background appear in black and white printouts:

Graph backgrounds may be printed as shades of gray and the darkness of the background color specified in the graph will be represented by a darker shade of the printed gray pattern. This option can be set in the *Print Options* dialog (see the first topic in this section).

How to use different fill patterns to print solid lines of different color:

This setting can be adjusted in the *Print Options* dialog (see the first topic in this section). The option

StatSoft™

to represent solid lines of different color as different patterns may produce desirable results when the lines to be printed are very thick (e.g., 5 points or more). This option is not recommended, however, to be used with thin lines because the differences in patterns representing different colors will not be salient enough to improve the readability of the differences between the lines, and at the same time the lines may appear jagged.

Are fonts set to specific sizes (in points) always printed having the requested *physical* sizes?

Dynamic image scaling in STATISTICA. In STATISTICA, all graph displays and printouts can be continuously scaled. STATISTICA will also automatically adjust the sizes of all fonts (proportionately to the overall size of the graph), such that manual adjustments of font sizes are never necessary.

The default printout size. Therefore, the fonts will be printed as having their specific *physical* sizes (as set in points; 1 point = $1/_{72}$ of an inch), only when the default printout size settings are used (and they can be printed smaller or larger depending on the requested printout size). Specifically, the fonts will appear printed in their exact *physical* size, for example:

This is 6 point

This is 8 point

This is 10 point

This is 12 point

This is 14 point

This is 16 point

if the letter-size paper is used, in portrait orientation with the default (1 inch) margins on all sides, and if the default graph proportions are not modified. The

manner in which the font size settings as requested in the graph translate into the actual physical sizes of the fonts which are displayed or printed can be globally adjusted using the *Global Font Decrease* or *Global Font Increase* buttons on the graphics toolbar (see the next topic).

How to quickly adjust (re-scale) sizes of all fonts in a graph:

A global font size adjustment facility is provided which will proportionately adjust the sizes of all fonts in a graph (both on the screen and in graph printouts). It can be enabled by pressing the *Global Font Decrease* or *Global Font Increase* buttons on the graphics toolbar (see page 64). This facility allows you to effectively increase or decrease all fonts not by changing the specific font size settings (e.g., not by changing an 8-point setting into a 12-point setting) but by globally adjusting the manner in which the logical font sizes are mapped into the plot region of the screen or the printout (see the previous topic for more information). Thus, after you press this button, a text in the graph which was set to size *8* (points) will remain set to *8*, but this size (*8*) will now be represented by approximately 20% larger letters when displayed or printed.

StatSoft™

Global Control of the Program and General User-Interface Conventions

What is the *Module Switcher* and how does it work?

As mentioned before, STATISTICA consists of modules, each containing a group of related procedures. When you switch modules, you can either keep STATISTICA down to one application window only, or alternatively, you can keep the previously-used modules open, because each of them can be run as a separate Windows application (see below).

All "general-purpose" facilities (such as the data spreadsheet and all graphics procedures) are available in every module and at every point of the analysis. The *Module Switcher* allows you to bring up another module from a list of all modules available in your version of STATISTICA.

The *Module Switcher* is similar to the Windows *Task Switcher* (which is called by double-clicking anywhere on the empty space on the Windows desktop) and can be invoked in a similar way, by double-clicking anywhere on the empty space within the STATISTICA application window. You can also call it by pressing the first button on every toolbar or by selecting the option *Other Statistics* in the pull-down menu *Analysis*.

The *Switcher* also allows you to review brief descriptions of statistical procedures and facilities included in each module (the summary descriptions on the right side of the window are updated as you scroll the list).

Two ways of bringing up new modules (the general mode of the *Switcher*). There are two different ways in which the *Module Switcher* can open new modules. Depending on the current configuration (see the *Defaults: General* option from the pull-down menu *Options*), it can open new modules into the same or new application windows.

(1) Single application mode. When you select the single application window mode, then switching between modules during a STATISTICA session will not open new application windows. Each new module will be opened into the same window replacing the module used before. Some users will like this "simple" mode because it keeps all analyses in a single application-window location and limits the number of programs opened on the desktop to the very minimum.

Note that a similar effect can be achieved by pressing the *End & Switch To* button in the *Module Switcher*; the application window of the current module will close but it will not be replaced by the new one, instead, the new module will open in the "next" application window.

(2) Multiple application mode. The main advantage of the multiple application mode is that you can run different analyses (modules) simultaneously in different, simultaneously open application windows. You can switch between the modules without closing the previous ones and take advantage of independent queues of Scrollsheets and graphs in different module windows.

This mode has clear advantages for most types of analyses allowing the user to use (and compare

results of) different analytic tools. Usually, it is not practical to keep more than four or five separate analyses open simultaneously (each with its own queue of Scrollsheets and graphs).

The maximum number of modules which can be simultaneously opened depends on the hardware and software resources of the computer (these resources can be monitored by selecting the *About...* option in the *Help* menu of the Windows *Program Manager*).

As a general rule, it is not recommended to open new applications when more than approximately 80% of Windows' resources are already used by programs which are currently running.

The selection of the operating mode can be made using the *Module Switching: Single Application Mode* setting, in the *Defaults: General* dialog (accessible from the pull-down menu *Options*). If the check box is marked, then STATISTICA will run in the single-application mode.

Customizing the list of modules in the Module Switcher.

Although the list of modules in the *Switcher* can be scrolled, it is convenient to have the modules most commonly used in your specific work listed on the top and thus not require scrolling; the order of modules listed can be customized by pressing the *Customize list...* button.

Note that the selection and order of modules listed in the *Switcher* is stored along with all other customizations of the STATISTICA system; thus you can maintain alternative lists for different projects.

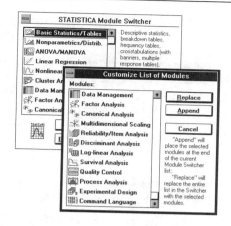

How to learn what information is necessary to start an analysis (variables, grouping codes, options, etc.):

Pressing *F1* will always open the relevant section of the on-line documentation containing a comprehensive explanation of all options in the current dialog. However, all analysis definition screens in STATISTICA follow the "self-prompting" dialog conventions. The *OK* button is never dimmed: whenever you are not sure what to select next, simply click *OK* (or press *O*) and the program will proceed to the next logical step and ask you for specific input if it is necessary.

What is the difference between the "floating" Cont (i.e., continue) button on the bottom of the screen and the Continue button in the upper left corner of a Scrollsheet or graph?

There is no difference between the functions of the two buttons as long as the number of Scrollsheets or graphs generated in one sequence by an analysis is not longer than the current "length of the queue" of

Scrollsheets or spreadsheets (by default 3, see page 97).

Descriptive Statistics [heart.sta]				
Continue...	Valid N	Mean	Minimum	Maximum
MONTH_1	65	6.07692	1.00000	12.00000
DAY_1	65	15.24615	2.00000	31.00000
YEAR_1	65	70.96923	68.00000	74.00000
MONTH_2	65	5.73846	1.00000	12.00000

Descriptive
Statistics

However, when more document windows are about to be generated than can fit in the current queue, then:

• pressing the *Continue* button on the Scrollsheet or graph will proceed with generating the consecutive Scrollsheets and graphs which are waiting in the sequence, while

• pressing the "floating" *Cont* button on the bottom of the screen--which, in fact, represents the iconized output selection dialog--will bring up the dialog, breaking the sequence of consecutive Scrollsheets or graphs.

Example. If the analysis you requested is about to create 10 separate histograms, and the current length of the queue of graphs is set to 3 (default), then STATISTICA will halt after the first 3 histograms are created, waiting for your signal to continue. Pressing the *Continue* button on the third histogram window will allow STATISTICA to continue with the next 3 graphs.

However, if instead of the *Continue* button on the graph, you press the "floating" *Cont* button on the bottom of the screen, the button will expand into the output selection dialog suppressing all (not yet displayed) graphs that STATISTICA was ready to produce.

What are the specific names of program files for individual modules of STATISTICA?

Here is an alphabetical list of program file names and applications (STATISTICA modules) which they represent.

reinst.exe   A STATISTICA re-installation utility (allowing you to install and remove modules of STATISTICA)

sta_bas.exe   Basic Statistics and Tables

sta_can.exe   Canonical Correlation Analysis

sta_clu.exe   Cluster Analysis Techniques

sta_com.exe   STATISTICA Command Language (SCL)

sta_dat.exe   Data Management module with the Quick MML programming language and the Megafile Manager data base management system

sta_dis.exe   Stepwise Discriminant Function Analysis with Classification of Cases

sta_exp.exe   Experimental Design Techniques (DOE)

sta_fac.exe   Factor Analysis Techniques

sta_log.exe   Log-linear Analysis Techniques

sta_man.exe   General ANOVA/MANOVA

sta_mul.exe   Multidimensional Scaling

sta_nln.exe   General Nonlinear Estimation, Logit and Probit Analysis

sta_non.exe   Nonparametric Statistics and Distribution Fitting

sta_pro.exe   Process Analysis Techniques

sta_qua.exe   Quality Control Charts

sta_reg.exe   Multiple Regression Techniques

StatSoft™

sta_rel.exe	Reliability and Item Analysis Techniques
sta_run.exe	STATISTICA "run" module (for creating "turn-key" applications)
sta_sur.exe	Survival and Failure Time Analysis Techniques
sta_tim.exe	Time Series Analysis and Forecasting
sta_win.exe	STATISTICA *Module Switcher*
stathelp.hlp	STATISTICA *electronic manual*

Note that when you create a new *Program Item* (icon) in a group on the Windows desktop, STATISTICA will automatically create the respective icon for the module and label it with an abbreviated name (no wider than the icon). If you find some of those names not sufficiently clear, you could edit or expand the name in the *Description* field of the Windows *Program Item Properties* dialog.

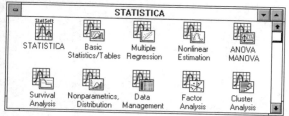

Refer to the section on *Icons representing modules* (page 22), and *Customizing STATISTICA* (page 1) for more information on running STATISTICA from custom application groups on the desktop.

Default file name extensions of files created by STATISTICA:

The default file name extensions for the four main types of files which STATISTICA uses most often are:

.sta	Spreadsheets (system data files)
.scr	Scrollsheets (scrollable tables with results)
.stg	Graphics files (including graph data and all graphic objects and customizations)
.sug	STATISTICA user-defined graph specification files (representing custom graphs added to the *Stats* pull-down menu)
.txt	Text (printout) output files and other supplementary files saved in the standard ASCII text format (e.g., multiple case selection condition files used in data recoding, frequency tables, multiple subset graphs, etc.)
.sel	Case selection conditions files
.csm	Macro files (recorded in STATISTICA)
.mfm	Megafile Manager data files
.qml	Quick MML program files
.mml	MML program files
.scl	STATISTICA Command Language files
.hlp	STATISTICA help files
.ini	STATISTICA configuration files
.pal	Color palette selection files

File name extensions for data and graphics files exchanged by STATISTICA with other applications:

.css	CSS (and STATISTICA/DOS) data files
.csg	CSS (and STATISTICA/DOS) graph files
.wmf	Windows graphics metafile files
.bmp	Windows device-independent bitmap graphics files
.xls	Excel worksheet files
.wk?, .wr?	Lotus, Symphony, and Quattro worksheet files (e.g., .wk1, .wk3)
.dbf	dBase files

StatSoft™

.db	Paradox files
.por	SPSS portable files
.fre	ASCII (free format text) files
.fix	ASCII (fixed format text) files

In some analyses, the *Results* summaries do not fit in their area (upper part) of the *Results* dialog. How can I review them?

This may happen when your Windows system is configured to use a large font as the default system font (e.g., the large font is used by default by some video drivers in the 800x600 mode). This font can be changed to the standard size either by switching to an alternative video driver provided with your video adapter or adjusting the driver configuration settings (refer to the driver documentation provided with your video adapter). On some systems, the adjustment can also be made using the Windows *Control Panel*. If you globally adjust the size of the Windows system font, then all your Windows applications will look more standard. If you prefer to maintain the current font as the system font in other applications, then you can configure this font locally in STATISTICA. To adjust the font size and/or style, press the *Dialog/Results* font button in the *Defaults: Display* dialog (option *Display...* in the pull-down menu *Options*).

The icons on buttons in STATISTICA dialogs are smaller than the space available on the buttons. How can I adjust them?

The reason for that is the larger default system font (as configured in your Windows system), which forces the buttons to a larger than standard size; all dialog buttons on such systems are larger. This fact is not easily noticeable in applications which (unlike STATISTICA) do not identify buttons with icons. If you prefer the appearance of STATISTICA dialogs as shown in the manual and the *Technical Description* brochure, adjust the current Windows system font (see the previous topic).

STATISTICA

INDEX

StatSoft™

Disk-output file vs. *Text/output Window*, 104
Displaying fitted functions (in graphs), 125
Double notation of values (summary), 9
Double notation of values (text/numeric), 89
Double-click on the cell, 80, 99
Double-click on the significant main effect (example), 19
Double-clicking on the status bar, 14
Drawing in zoom mode, 56
Dynamic image scaling in graphs, 139
Dynamic mode (in graphs), 52
Dynamic output tables, 13

E

Edit Palette dialog, 129
Editing cells, 80
Embedding or linking mode (in graphs), 61
End & Switch To button in the *Module Switcher*, 29, 140
Error bar drawing mode, 60
Excel (interface with), 92
Export data, 93

F

F2 (edit cell), 80, 99
File headers, 87
File information/notes, 87
File manager, 94
File name extensions, 143
Fill block, 87
Fill Down and *Fill Right* options, 87
Fill ranges of cells in spreadsheets, 86
Fitted function equations in *Stats Graphs*, 126
Fitting functions (in graphs), 125
Fixed mode (in graphs), 52
Floating *Cont* button, 141
Footnotes in graphs, 124
Foreign data files, 93
Formulas in the spreadsheet, 81
Four main types of document windows in STATISTICA (MDI), 25
Free-hand/polyline/polygon drawing mode, 59

G

G/L and *P/L* buttons (*Graph Data Editor*), 116
General default settings, 30
General Layout dialog, 118
Global case editing/restructuring options, 35
Global column width adjustment (in spreadsheets), 36
Global Font Decrease tool (in graphs), 64
Global Font Increase tool (in graphs), 64
Global variable editing/restructuring options, 34
Global vs. Clipboard operations on cases, 35
Global vs. Clipboard operations on variables, 34
Global vs. Clipboard-based operations, 92
Graph Data Editor, 115
Graph Data Editor (button), 53
Graph default settings, 30
Graph printout settings, 137
Graph queues, 112
Graph vs. plot, 115
Graphic Text Editor, 57
Graphics file format, 112
Gridlines in output and the speed of printing, 72
Gridlines in tables, 102, 104

H

Headers, comments, 10
Help system and on-line manual, 16

I

Icons representing STATISTICA modules, 22
Import (data) facilities, 92
Individual users on a network, 32
Information/notes stored with data files, 87
Install and remove modules of STATISTICA, 142
Installation procedure, 11
Integration between the documents, 25
Internal batch processing mode, 24
Interrupting analyses, 70

L

Left-mouse-button (in graphs), 118
Left-mouse-button vs. right-mouse-button (in graphs), 118
Length of the queues, 98
Line shape editing mode (in graphs), 60
Line style (in graphs), 62
Line thickness in graph printouts, 138
Linking STATISTICA graph files via OLE, 132
Linking vs. embedding (overview), 61
Links between files (DDE), 87
Links manager (DDE), 88
Linking mode (in graphs), 61
Locking and saving graphs, 112
Locking and saving Scrollsheets, 98
Log of Scrollsheets, 67
Logical vs. physical font sizes (in graphs), 64
Logical zoom (in graphs), 55
Loops in Quick MML, 82

M

Macro status field (status bar), 74
Macros, 26
Magnifying glass (in graphs), 56
Main components of the interactive user-interface in STATISTICA, 21
Maintaining the graph aspect ratio, 55
Make Scrollsheet... option, 97
Manual vs. Auto scaling (in graphs), 121
Manual/0 vs. Auto/0 scaling (in graphs), 121
Mapping font sizes onto plot regions of different sizes (in graphs), 64
MAR (Maintain Aspect Ratio) mode (in graphs), 54
Margin width (in Scrollsheets), 45
Margins, 71, 101
Margins within the graph area, 120
Mark (un-marks) values (in Scrollsheets), 45
Marked values in the *Graph Data Editor*, 46, 116
Matrix input data, 94
Mean, standard deviations, standard errors statistics, 91
Megafile Manager, 95
Merging long value labels, 80
Message area of the status bar, 71

StatSoft™

StatSoft™